FOUNDATIONS FOR A SOCIAL THEOLOGY:
PRAXIS, PROCESS AND SALVATION

DERMOT A. LANE

FOUNDATIONS
FOR A
SOCIAL THEOLOGY:
PRAXIS,
PROCESS AND
SALVATION

PAULIST PRESS
NEW YORK · RAMSEY

Published in the United States by
Paulist Press
545 Island Road
Ramsey, N.J. 07446
© Dermot A. Lane 1984
ISBN 0-8091-2622-2
Library of Congress Catalog Card Number: 83-62948
Print origination in Ireland by
Galaxy Reproductions Limited
Printed in Hong Kong

*Dedicated to
My Mother and Father,
living examples of Christian praxis*

Contents

Acknowledgments

Most of the research that went into the writing of this book was done while on sabbatical in North America from September 1981 to August 1982. I wish therefore to thank in the first place my Ordinary, Dermot Ryan, Archbishop of Dublin, for granting me leave from teaching responsibilities and for supporting me throughout that year.

During my year of study I was fortunate to enjoy the hospitality and fellowship of different Institutions of learning. Foremost among these was the theological community of The Catholic University of America, Washington D.C., who under the auspices of the Department of Religion and Religious Education, from January 1982 to June 1982, accorded me a warm welcome and many stimulating discussions. I also spent time in the autumn of 1981 in Toronto studying at St Michael's College while residing with the community of St Basil. Thirdly, I finished up my sabbatical during the summer of 1982 among the Society of St Edmund at St Michael's College, Winooski, Vermont. To all three Institutions, I now wish, some eighteen months later, to express formally my gratitude for much kindness and gracious hospitality.

Being on sabbatical creates problems back home. Someone else has to carry the lecture load. To all in Clonliffe College and Mater Dei Institute of Education who so willingly carried my work-load I wish to express much thanks.

The writing of a book is made possible only by the encouragement of others. These I also wish to thank and I hope that they will forgive me for not mentioning all their names here. In particular, I wish to thank Dr Donal Murray,

Auxiliary to the Archbishop of Dublin, and Sr Bernard Boran, Mater Dei Institute of Education, both of whom read the manuscript in its entirety and made valuable suggestions. The final outcome of the book is, however, my own responsibility, and whatever flaws remain, remain as mine only.

A special word of thanks is due to my typist. Mrs Maura Purcell, the Secretary of Mater Dei Institute of Education, who typed and re-typed, with great patience, many different drafts.

Lastly, I wish to record my thanks to the publishers Gill & Macmillan, Dublin, and Paulist Press, New Jersey, U.S.A. Both Michael Gill of Gill & Macmillan and Jean Marie Hiesberger of Paulist Press made constructive suggestions in the course of bringing this manuscript into book form.

Dermot A. Lane
September, 1983
Mater Dei Institute of Education
Clonliffe Road
Dublin 3

Foundations for a Social Theology:
Praxis, Process and Salvation

Introduction

We are living in an era of extraordinary social, political and cultural change. These changes are marked by the creation of great divisions and deep conflicts among people in society. Injustices, violence and disregard of human rights abound all around us. The world we live in has become a daily theatre of war: the Middle East, central America, Northern Ireland ... The future of the human race is threatened by nuclear destruction.

Yet in spite of this desperate picture of life today, all people, black and white, male and female, rich and poor, strong and weak, are united in a common search for healing and wholeness. The aim of this book is to show in some small way that Christianity has within itself a vision and praxis that can contribute significantly to this common quest for unity, reconciliation and human development.

Until fairly recently the impression was often given that Christian faith was a highly private affair. Christianity seemed to be a religion concerned primarily with the development of 'individual' faith, the elimination of 'personal' sin, and the promotion of the salvation of 'my' soul. These are important elements in the Christian message, but it must be stated explicitly that they are by no means the whole story, or indeed the centrepiece of the gospel of Jesus Christ.

Today, we know only too well in the light of the behavioural sciences that the individual is never merely an individual. He or she belongs to a social network of human relationships. The individual is always an individual in relation to a community: family, friends, and country. The individual is radically social.

In an even more profound sense the Christian is a thoroughly social human being. Being a Christian involves belonging to that larger reality we call the People of God. It also entails membership of that organic entity we call the Body of Christ. Christianity is essentially a social religion and as such has important social implications. The working out of some of these social implications is the task of social theology.

This book sets out to indicate the general direction that a contemporary social theology might take. It shows how 'individual' faith can exist only in a community of faith, how 'personal' sin is tied up with structural sin and how the salvation of 'my' soul takes place only in reference to the salvation of others. In particular this book seeks to establish the close relationship that exists between religion and politics, God and society, social analysis and theology, faith and praxis, liberation and salvation, eucharist and justice.

In working out the contours of a contemporary social theology one must make certain judgments about basic foundational issues: the source of knowledge and truth (epistemology), the nature of reality (ontology), the composition of human identity (anthropology). There was a time in theology when agreed answers to these questions could be taken for granted. This is no longer the case. It is now an open secret that the burning issues in theology today are in origin foundational issues. The so-called crisis in theology is not theological but philosophical at base. For this reason it is essential today in theology, especially as it moves into the public forum of social questions, that it give a credible account of its underlying foundational suppositions.

This book claims to deal with *some* of the basic foundational principles that might be used in the construction of a social theology. It examines the source of human knowledge and truth. It notes that the classical view suggests that knowledge and truth are derived from the contemplation of the world *as it is*. Knowledge and truth are essentially contemplative in origin. Truth is to be found in some kind of correspondence between the mind and reality (*adequatio rei et mentis*). Another view, however, proposes that knowledge and truth are given to us in the experience of changing the world from the way it is to the way it should be in the light of God's revelation. Knowledge and truth are presented as bound up with action and performance. Clearly the particular model of knowledge and truth that social theology adopts will be of the utmost importance. This particular question is faced squarely in the course of this book.

Equally important, at the foundational level, is the particular paradigm of reality that social theology adopts. If reality is seen as something static, fixed and closed, then social theology will take a very definite direction. If, on the other hand, reality is perceived as dynamic, open and unfinished, then social theology will move in an entirely different direction. Something of a tension seems to exist between these two possible ways of perceiving reality. This tension was picked up at the Second Vatican Council which pointed out:

> ... the human race has passed from a rather static concept of reality, to a more dynamic, evolutionary one. In consequence there has arisen a new series of problems, a series as important as can be, calling for a new effort of analysis and synthesis.
>
> (*Gaudium et Spes*, a.5)

This shift from a static view of reality to a more dynamic one requires a new philosophical framework. Some suggestions are made in the light of contemporary movements in the new physics, feminism, philosophy, and ecology, as to how this new understanding of reality might be developed in the service of a social theology.

The third foundational issue to be touched upon concerns the composition of human identity. Here it is suggested that more attention should be given to the individual as a being who becomes, in contrast to the individual as a being who simply is. The individual as a being-in-becoming develops to a large degree by what he or she does. In a very real sense the individual is what he or she freely chooses to do. In an equally important sense the individual can only do what he or she is called and enabled to do within community. This delicate relationship between being and becoming within the constitution of human identity is explored within the larger context of the demands of a social theology.

In the light of these foundational issues it could be said that the backbone of this book is praxis, process, and salvation. Praxis is about creative action, inspired by critical reflection, that gives rise to both change and insight. Within this perspective praxis is the ground, source and goal of theory. Process is about the dynamic, relational and organic character of all reality. According to a process view of the world, emphasis is placed on the primacy of becoming within being and the possibilities this opens up for Christian praxis.

Salvation is the goal of all theology, especially social theology. As such, salvation is not simply a theory about life but primarily an experience to be lived and a task to be performed under God's gracious offer of new life in Christ. The underlying thesis of this book is that social theology is about the creative interplay of praxis and process in the promotion of salvation.

Finally, this book does not claim in any sense to provide all the foundations necessary for a social theology, nor does it pretend to present a complete social theology. Its goal is much more modest. It merely seeks to initiate a discussion about these complex issues at a time when the world is desperately in need of new direction. This book is written in the conviction that something can be done to overcome the serious social divisions and conflicts that exist in our world today. There is a growing fatalism abroad that needs to be countered by a renewed optimism. This sense of fatalism overcome by optimism is delicately captured by the Irish poet Derek Mahon:

'The world is everything that is the case'
From the fly giving up in the coal shed
To the Winged Victory of Samothrace.
Give blame, praise, to the fumbling God
Who hides, shame-facedly, His aged face;
Whose light retires behind its veil of cloud.

The world, though, is also so much more –
Everything that is the case imaginatively.
Tacitus believed mariners could hear
The sun sinking into the western sea;
And who would question that titanic roar,
The steam rising wherever the edge may be?

('Tractatus' in *Courtyards in Delft*,
Dublin: Gallery Books, 1981)

The purpose of this book is to recover, in the spirit of a Tacitus, a sense of optimism in the midst of so much fatalism by appealing to the imaginative vision and praxis of the Christian message.

1

The Move to Praxis in Theology

Anyone looking in from the outside at what has been going on inside Christianity could hardly fail to be impressed by the extraordinary advances which have taken place in the latter half of this century. These developments have occurred not only in theology but also in Church life. An outline of the theological and ecclesial achievements would include at least the following historical realities: the Second Vatican Council , the Lambeth Conferences, *Populorum Progressio*, CELAM I and II, Faith and Order Conferences, Ecumenical agreed Statements, and the recent Lima Agreement (1982). Only the cynic would deny that something highly creative is taking place inside the theological and ecclesial communities of faith.

At the same time, however, it must be admitted that these quite extraordinary achievements have very little real impact on public life. The so-called real world of economics, politics, and culture have remained relatively untouched by these theological developments and ecclesial events. The fact of the matter is that these advances, however admirable in themselves, appear to our imaginary outsider friend as rather cerebral, highly academic, and purely theoretical as achievements. Life goes on as before and there seems to be very little difference, if indeed any, in the social character and structure of christian existence in the light of these developments. As one US bishop recently remarked in reference to the social teaching of the Church: 'The "trickle-down" theory seems to have sprung a leak'.[1] The dreams and visions of the Second Vatican Council have not caught on in the way one would have expected among the people of God, though there have been some notable exceptions in the area of liturgy. Enthusiasm for the ecumenical movement has been dampened and expectations have been reduced in spite of the recent remark by one observer about the Lima Agreement that if a man and a woman had said the things the Churches said on that extraordinary occasion, without subsequently getting married, then one or other party could sue. A growing gap exists between pastoral practice and established theological conclusions The agreed teachings of the Churches are by no means evenly accepted on the ground by the pilgrim people of God. Something seriously wrong seems to have taken place somewhere along the line in spite of so much theological progress.

To be sure, there are many good things going on in the Churches and taking place in theological circles that do make a real difference in life and yet never seem to make 'the news'. However, in proportion to the massive theoretical gains that exist 'on paper' in theology and 'in the books' of the Churches, the overall effect on the ground in real life and in social practice is disturbingly scant. A glaring discrepancy does exist between theory and practice, faith and experience, life and religion.

Western theology, by and large, has been too preoccupied with what David Tracy aptly describes as 'the cognitive identity crisis of the contents of faith of Christianity in modernity'.[2] Christianity seems to be concerned primarily with theoretical issues about belief and truth within its own household. Christian faith is still described too frequently as an intellectual assent to a body of truths handed down from one generation to the next generation. Special attention continues to be given as a priority to safeguarding the intellectual integrity of the deposit of faith in its transmission. This overall focus and particular emphasis accounts to some extent for the slight impact of traditional Christianity upon social and historical realities in our world today.

Something of a reaction to this tendency towards the purely theoretical and conceptual within Christianity has been taking place in the last twenty-five years. This reaction can be found in the emergence of what has come to be known as European political theology and Latin-American liberation theology. It is not my intention here to map out the developments of these theologies. This is something that has already been done more ably by others.[3] Instead, we will focus attention on the existence of an underlying common bond between these two different schools of theology.[4] This bond is the existence of a radical turn towards praxis that can be found as a focal point in both political and liberation theology. This turn to praxis is one response, among others, to the serious cleavage that exists between theological achievements and pastoral practice within the Church today. It should be noted at this early stage that the expressions 'the turn to praxis' and its corollary 'the primacy of praxis in theology' are technical expressions which we hope will become clear in the course of this book.

The purpose of this chapter is to explore this turn to praxis and its significance for the future of Christianity in its public relationship to society. Political and liberation theology are not just new segments, as it were, to be conveniently added on to traditional theology. Rather they are new ways of doing theology that affect the whole enterprise of theology. In particular the turn to praxis, common in these two theologies, is in fact the centrepiece of a new style of theologising. This turn to praxis, as we shall see, is a corrective to the apparent theoretical one-sidedness of much Christian theology and its seeming social innocence and public ineffectiveness. The turn to praxis is ultimately a methodological issue, calling for a break with one particular way of doing theology, in the hope of recovering another, older style of theology, more characteristic of the early Church.

By way of preliminary introduction to the turn to praxis it should be noted that this development is part of two other significant turns that have been taking place in theology in this century. The first of these is the turn to experience. The discovery of experience as a basic source of theology was an important step on the way to praxis. Once theology rediscovered its foothold in experience, as it did formally at the Second Vatican Council, it was simply a matter of time, in fact only a few years, before praxis would move to the centre of the stage.[5] Praxis is an extension of the experiential base of theology; praxis is the application of the principle of experience to the realm of transforming activity; praxis is a particular form of human experience; praxis is the experience of reflective activity. As we shall see in the course of this book many of the basic principles governing the use of experience as a source in theology also apply to praxis.

The second significant turn facilitating this emerging emphasis on praxis concerns the turn to the subject.[6] Here the individual is regarded no longer as object but as subject. Humanity is understood from 'the inside out' and not from 'the outside in'. Human identity, dignity and agency reside in the subjectivity of the individual. The development of the person as subject takes place, on the individual and social planes, not only in conjunction with other subjects but also in relation to God, the Supreme Subject who graciously enables all subjects to be fully human subjects. The individual as subject is always a free subject, assuming personal responsibility for his or her actions in the world. When we talk about praxis we are always talking about the praxis of a free responsible subject who participates in the shaping of her/his own historical destiny. Further, as we shall see, the praxis of the subject is something that affects other subjects; the praxis of the subject is never innocent but always part of a larger network of social and organic relationships. These different turns — the turn to experience, the turn to the subject, and the turn to praxis — constitute together a single significant shift, indeed some would say a revolution, taking place in contemporary theology. Our concern here is to focus specifically on the turn to praxis by taking into account the turns to experience and to the subject that have already been achieved. In this sense the emergence of praxis as central to theology is the outcome of the other two developments. In the light of this introduction we can now take up the turn to praxis in political and liberation theology.

Praxis and Political Theology

The development of the place of praxis in political theology has been undertaken most explicitly by Johann B. Metz.[7] In discussing this turn to praxis, Metz distinguishes two phases of development in his own thinking. He openly acknowledges that it was only after the first stage of the development of political theology which he dates around 1969 that he began to take seriously the primacy of praxis in theology. In the light of critical work by many of his students Metz began to realise after 1969 'the practical limitations of a purely theoretical critical theology'.[8] These limitations forced him to develop a fundamental practical theology in which he explicitly affirms the primacy of praxis as distinct from and in contrast to a purely theoretical theology. The best way to appreciate this later development in Metz's theology is to situate it against his criticism of Karl Rahner and Wolfhart Pannenberg.

Metz claims that Christianity is at present undergoing a serious historical crisis of identity. This crisis is symbolised by the emergence of what is often referred to as the post-Christian or post-religious world in which we are presently living. The theories put forward that are most acceptable in coping with this particular crisis are what Metz calls 'the transcendental and idealistic theories of Christianity'. These theories are to be found in the universal, historical theology of W. Pannenberg and the transcendental theology of K. Rahner.[9]

Pannenberg works out an ontology of history and meaning that is exclusively the product of reflection. In this theory, history is the bearer of meaning; meaning is anticipated in Jesus; and this meaning will be fully realised eschatologically at the end of time. As such this understanding of history bears no relation to practical reason and does not take any account of subsequent events in history says Metz. Most of all this is a highly idealistic vision of history that is not in touch with the harsh realities of life.[10]

As for Rahner's transcendental theology, Metz argues in general terms that the concept of experience employed by Rahner does not take adequate account of historical experience which carries so much suffering, antagonism and social contradictions. Further, transcendental theology tends to over-legitimise the identity of the religious subject in a world that is fraught with too much suffering.[11] In particular, Metz criticises Rahner's transcendental theology of anonymous Christianity. This theory of Rahner is put forward to meet the crisis of identity within Christianity with a view to accounting for the fact that so many exist outside the Church or do not believe in God. In response to this Rahner argues for a view of the individual as a dynamic being who is orientated in and through human transcendence towards God. Each human being is graced by God from the very beginning of existence, even though he/she may not recognise this gift. Every person, in a manner of speaking, is 'condemned in transcendence' and is 'always already with God'. According to Metz, Rahner's theology of anonymous Christianity bears the marks of a certain élitism. Only a privileged few really know the true situation of humanity, even though this kind of élitism is not in keeping with Rahner's basic theological principles. In addition, Metz points out that in this transcendental understanding of Christianity, the identity of faith is fixed according to a basic anthropological structure according to which the person is 'always already with God' whether he/she wants to be or not. The real difficulty with this position is that it does not seem to recognise that this basic anthropological structure which exists in history can itself be threatened by history.[12]

Metz very graphically and colourfully illustrates his criticism of Rahner by recounting a famous German fairytale about the hedgehog and the hare:

One Sunday morning, the hedgehog is going for a walk in a ploughed field and a hare teases him about his bandy legs. He challenges the hare to a race in the furrow of the field. First however, he goes home to breakfast because, as he tells the hare, he cannot run on an empty stomach. He then returns with his wife, who is exactly the same in appearance as her husband, and gets her to stand at the far end of the furrow. He himself stands at the other end beside the hare in another furrow. The hare falls for this trick. He runs and runs in his furrow but the hedgehog is (in both positions) 'always already there'. In the end the hare falls dead from exhaustion on the field.[13]

In one particular version of this fairytale the hedgehog trick stands for the transcendental understanding of the identity of Christianity. The two hedgehogs are 'always already there' and as such they harass the poor hare who runs and runs, by simply announcing alternately 'I am already here.' Because each hedgehog is exactly the same, 'the beginning is like the end, creation is like fulfilment, and at the end the beginning repeats itself'. Once again the identity of the subject of Christian faith is cut off from the obvious threats that exist in history. The human subject is immunised from the real hazards of history. The intrinsic demands of Christian faith to reform history and indeed to change the course of history in the name of apocalypse and eschatology are ignored and broken off prematurely. In short Metz argues that the transcendental and idealist approaches to Christianity do not take history 'with all its contradictions, antagonisms, struggles and sufferings seriously' enough with the result that they end up making an 'as if' issue out of the conflicts of history.[14]

In contrast to these idealistic and transcendental approaches to Christian identity, Metz briefly outlines the possibility of another quite different point of departure for Christian theology. This starting point he calls 'a practical fundamental theology which understands itself as a political theology . . . characterised by a cognitive primacy of praxis, i.e. by the dialectic of theory and praxis'.[15] He suggests that a 'historical praxis of opposition to meaninglessness and an absence of salvation' is 'indispensable' to the identity of Christian faith and that a theology of the one, universal history of salvation must take account of 'the heads of the people who are bowed down under their own histories of suffering'. The offer of salvation in Christianity 'does not become universal via an idea, but via the intelligible power of a praxis, the praxis of following Christ. This intelligibility of Christianity cannot be transmitted theologically in a purely speculative way.'[16] Further, Metz argues that the 'meaning of history' which is so important in theology cannot be taken unthinkingly by theologians out of the treasure chest of ontology without first of all being introduced by the creative force of Christian action.[17] In brief, 'the so-called historical crisis of identity of Christianity is not a crisis of the contents of faith, but rather a crisis . . . of the practical meaning of those contents, the imitation of Christ.'[18] This rather condensed account of Metz in his own words of an alternative approach to theology must now be unpacked and elaborated. This can be done by looking at the overall thrust of his plea for a practical fundamental theology.

The first point to note about Metz's proposal for a practical fundamental theology is that he is using the terms theory and praxis in a very definite, specific and technical sense. For most people praxis is regarded as the continuation, implementation or concrete application of a previously defined theory. In such instances praxis is subordinate to theory. Metz wishes to move away from this more traditional approach to theology. He proposes instead that there should be a dialectical relation between theory and praxis, and that within this dialectical relation primacy should be given to praxis. This praxis, of course, is always a reflective praxis; it is never simply praxis divorced from theory. Inspired by theory, praxis discloses its own intelligible perspectives. The experience of praxis is therefore an important source of human understanding. In this particular sense, practical fundamental theology is subject to the primacy of praxis. Attempts to base theology exclusively on pure theory or absolute reflection are judged by Metz to be uncritical and turn out to be merely academic constructs.[19]

Metz justifies this emphasis on praxis by appealing to the practical implications of the Christian message. The Christian concept of God is a highly practical one. The God of Jesus Christ is a God who stirs up and encroaches on the practical interest of the person who is trying to think of Him. The reality of God is one that disarms yet enlivens, haunts yet heals, disturbs and yet enables. The practical realities of conversion and exodus are intrinsic to the experience of God; they are not just dramatic embellishments of a previously worked-out 'pure' theology.

In particular, christological knowledge contains within itself a practical structure which Metz sums up in terms of the praxis of the imitation of Christ. It is only when people begin to imitate Christ in praxis that they know who it is to whom they have given their allegiance. In this regard Metz faults modern christologies for not bringing out the practical structure of christology, for adopting a non-dialectical relationship between theory and praxis, and therefore for remaining too idealistic.[20] The New Testament stories about Jesus contain within themselves a strong thrust towards praxis. In other words we should not distinguish too sharply between narrative and commandment in the Gospel accounts as if we first of all hear the story of Jesus and then subsequently decide in reflection what to do.

In the light of these remarks Metz proceeds to explain the difference between his earlier and later political theology. He acknowledges that even in his earlier formulation of political theology he had taken the primacy of praxis as a point of departure. However, the reason why this did not succeed as much as it might have is that the concept of praxis he was using had too much content and therefore was open to misunderstanding. On the one hand Metz wants to affirm that 'the primacy of praxis in philosophy (Kant, the enlightenment — Marx) should be regarded as the real Copernican revolution in philosophy' that enables us to do theology in the real, practical world in contrast to the world merely made up of ideas.[21] At the same time, however, he wishes to make an important distinction between moral *practice* in Kant and social praxis according to Marx, a distinction he now readily admits he failed to bring out adequately in his earlier political theology. In Kant, the practice in question is individual moral practice enlightened by the primacy of practical reason:

> Individual moral imperatives in Kant's teaching replace the question of social action and conceal the fact that coming of age is a question not only of the moral exertion of the individual but of social structures and relationships.[22]

The challenge of the enlightenment for Kant, the coming

of age for modern man/woman, was to make the individual free from the blind forces of nature, history and authority in the exercise of his/her practical reason. However, Kant failed to realise that individual moral action is insufficient to deal with the structural elements of human oppression. In particular, Kant did not take account of the fact that individual moral praxis is by no means socially innocent or politically neutral. It was Marx who brought out the fact that individual moral actions affect the character of 'social structures and relationships'. Marx highlighted that these 'structures and relationships' could be changed and so issued a radical call for the new social praxis. What Kant failed to bring out was that much of the alienation in the world today is not simply the result of moral weakness or human failure on the part of individuals; it is quite often, as Marx emphasised, the result of larger structural and social conditions which must become the object of social praxis. In other words, it was Marx who highlighted that the evil which needs to be overcome in the world today is not just the evil of a few individuals but also the structural evil of the system as a whole. Consequently, it is not enough to engage simply in individual moral practice, we must also be prepared to adopt a social praxis, that goes beyond individual acts and addresses collectively the social and structural conditions of life.

According to Metz an essential part of the challenge of the Enlightenment has still to be met by theology in so far as there are people who are oppressed in a manner that does not result simply from human frailty but is caused by a larger social reality. This remaining but essential part of the challenge of the Enlightenment can only be met in theology by a creative, social praxis. Christian praxis 'must be concerned not only with man's (woman's) state as a subject in the presence of God but also with the fact that men (women) can become subjects and live as subjects rising from misery and oppression.'[23] Theology, therefore, must include not only moral practice but also social praxis as a form of behaviour intrinsic to *metanoia*, exodus and the imitation of Christ.

Having established the importance of Christian praxis as a

social praxis, Metz suggests three basic characteristics of Christian praxis. In the first place Christian praxis as social must always be ethically determined. The purpose of this qualification is to ensure that the praxis in question will not lead to an abstract or violent negation of the individual. This consideration and requirement is extremely important in view of the fact that often the demands made by social praxis forget about the absoluteness of the individual. Secondly, Christian praxis as a social praxis should be influenced by the memory of the Gospel story. Here Metz has in mind that form of memory which can function as a disturbing reality within society. Without this reference to memory, especially the liberating memory of Jesus, there is a real danger that our social praxis will be influenced by the prevailing social outlook and so simply end up reproducing the dominant social viewpoint. Thirdly, Christian praxis as social praxis must embody a structure of empathy which acts as a form of opposition to the present-day apathy of society. Metz's favourite example of this empathic involvement within praxis is the principle of solidarity, especially solidarity with the dead and past victims of injustice. This solidarity within praxis is also another form of memory. As such this principle of solidarity within praxis guards against any easy understanding of the history of suffering in terms of evolution or dialectics.[24] In developing these three points Metz is also arguing over his shoulder against certain forms of modern critical theory in Germany.

Some initial and preliminary reaction to Metz's proposals on praxis must be made at this stage before moving on to look at liberation theology. His basic thesis on praxis is both subtle and sophisticated. As such, it is an important contribution towards a theology of the practical dimension of Christian faith. Clearly he is not advocating an irresponsible dismissal of the role of reason or a new kind of mindless activism. To the contrary, his proposals are an explicit check against and refutation of this obvious temptation in religion. Metz is only too well aware of the possibility that the turn to praxis will be seized upon by some as an excuse for opting out of and abandoning the essential task of providing constructive, intellectual, and theoretical backing for Christian praxis. Instead, he is positing a complex, creative and dialectical relationship between theory and praxis. Within this dialectical relationship, it is praxis that exercises a critical control on the claims of reason. At this level alone, Metz has provided in a tantalisingly brief and at times frustratingly condensed form the basis of a much-needed new criterion for the validity of theological discourse and pastoral activity. In doing so he has hinted at the outlines of an epistemology that seem, at first glance, to be more in keeping with the biblical, theological and eschatological perceptions of truth than most traditional and classical epistemologies, a point we shall take up again later on. His remarks about the Enlightenment and the distinction between moral practice and social praxis, and the challenge that these still present for theology, are as provocative as they are constructive for the preservation of a credible contemporary Christian faith. While it is true that Christianity has come to grips to some extent with the cognitive crisis of identity posed by the Enlightenment, Metz has shown how it still remains an urgent task for the Church to cope with the socio-ethical-political problems posed by the Enlightenment in terms of working out a practical theology of Christian faith, i.e. a theology of Christian praxis. The link up between his proposal on the theory-praxis relationship with theological and christological knowledge provide an important clue as to how Christianity might once again regain its lost social and political significance in the world today. His efforts to recover memory and solidarity as basic categories within Christian social praxis have ties with what is best in the Christian tradition: memoria, the unity of the Body of Christ, the communion of saints, the groaning of creation, and the promise of a new heaven and a new earth. These highly suggestive ideas of Metz will be unpacked later on in chapters two and three.

On the debit side it has to be pointed out that Metz's constructive and creative proposals require more philosophical elaboration and theological backing if they are to succeed. To be specific it must be stated that narrative alone, even though it does implicitly contain a praxis-imperative, is not enough. The story of Jesus must be told and re-told in a way that specifically addresses the experiences, individual, social and political of the contemporary situation and overtly animates responsible praxis. This will not happen automatically without some form of critical correlation with and creative insertion into the experiential and social circumstances of the day. This point of entry by narrative into the contemporary social world requires at least some form of concrete social analysis of the human situation through the aid of the social sciences — something to which Metz does not seem to give adequate attention. Secondly, there is no reason why, as others have already suggested, Rahner's transcendental theology and Metz's political theology cannot be dialectically integrated in a way that would be mutually enriching to both perspectives.[25] The universal claims of Rahner's transcendental theology need to be mediated by Metz's political theology and the particularity of political theology demands the universal dimension of Rahner's transcendental theology. The concreteness of political activity needs to be nourished by a transcendental orientation if it is to be viable. Equally the grace of transcendence needs to be incarnated in personal, social and political forms if it is to remain alive and visible in our contemporary world. Thirdly, one must wonder how fair is Metz in his criticism of Rahner. Is it true to say that Rahner, who has written so persuasively on themes like the turn to experience and the subject, the unity between love of God and love of neighbour, the Church as social critic, the Marxist-Christian dialogue ... is insensitive to the demands of history and politics? After all, Rahner does readily admit that 'theology must be 'political' theology'[26] even though he does not spell out the implications of this statement. Lastly, it does not seem wholly accurate to suggest that *all* modern christologies have neglected the practical character of the mystery of Christ. The works of L. Boff, I. Sobrino, and E. Schillebeeckx are clear exceptions to this perhaps otherwise largely valid criticism.[27]

Praxis and Liberation Theology

Like political theology, liberation theology also gives a prominent place to praxis in its own self-understanding. Most descriptions of liberation theology contain reference at some stage to the importance of praxis. Probably the most sophisticated account of liberation theology is to be found in the writings of Gustavo Gutiérrez. We will, therefore, focus our attention on his contribution to the place of praxis in liberation theology.

In his highly acclaimed book *A Theology of Liberation*, Gutiérrez outlines a series of new emphases in theology which show 'that communion with the Lord inescapably means a Christian life centred around concrete and creative commitment of service to others'.[28] It is this commitment in love to the service of others, especially the poor, that makes up the heart of liberation theology. The new emphases bringing about this orientation include:

— a rediscovery of charity as the centre of the Christian life,

— the unification of contemplation and action in
                                                    spirituality,

— a greater sensitivity to the anthropological aspects of
                                                    revelation,

— Church life as a *locus theologicus*,

— Vatican II theology of the signs of the times,

— the importance of action for reflection,

— the Christian-Marxist dialogue,

— the recovery of the eschatological dimension of
                                                    theology.[29]

These different factors, in addition to highlighting the practical character of theology, have given rise to a new understanding of the critical function of theology.

Gutiérrez begins by describing theology as 'a critical reflection on Christian praxis in the light of the Word'. This critical function of theology extends to economic, social and cultural issues, society and Church, the theory of theology itself as linked to praxis, the pastoral action of the Church, and historical events. This does not mean that theology as wisdom and rational knowledge is now ignored. It does demand, however, that theological 'wisdom and knowledge will . . . have ecclesiastical praxis as their point of departure'. For Gutiérrez liberation theology is 'not so much a new theme for reflection as a new way to do theology'.[30] It is a new way of doing theology in so far as he is suggesting that theology is basically a critical reflection on the Christian praxis of liberation. As such, it is a 'second step' reflection which arises, as Hegel used to say of philosophy, 'only at sundown'. This preliminary description of theology by Gutiérrez is developed and nuanced in subsequent articles, especially 'Liberation Praxis and Christian Faith'.[31]

What emerges in these subsequent articles by Gutiérrez is that theology operates out of a prior commitment to the poor. The basic point of departure for theology is involvement with the oppressed. Thus Gutiérrez writes:

. . . liberation theology comes up only after
                    involvement. . . .[32]

Liberation theology has maintained that active
    commitment to liberation comes first, theology develops
                    from it.[33]

It is this emphasis on a prior commitment as the pre-condition of theology that prompts Gutiérrez to point out that theologians themselves must be involved in the process of liberation if their work is to be concrete and scientific.[34]

This prior commitment to the cause of the poor is designated as praxis and here Gutiérrez means by praxis the unity that obtains between reflection and action. He describes this praxis sometimes as historical praxis and other times as social praxis. Either way it is specified as a praxis of liberation which 'implies identification with oppressed human beings and social classes and solidarity with their interests and struggles'. It is from this particular perspective and prior commitment to the process of liberation that we can now begin to understand the full significance of what Gutiérrez means by saying that theology is a critical reflection on praxis in the light of the Word of God. One of the purposes of this critical reflection is that it will 'help to make this commitment more radical and complete'.[35] In fact Gutiérrez says explicitly: 'Liberation theology wants to help to make that process (i.e. the prior commitment to the liberation of the poor) more self-critical and hence more comprehensive and radical'.[36] It does this by showing, for example, that political involvement with liberation is part of (note not identical with) the wider and deeper reality of Christ's gratuitous gift of total liberation. Further, this critical reflection in the light of the gospel helps to change the prior commitment of liberating praxis into a praxis of love addressed to our neighbour and therefore to Christ who identified himself with the least of humanity.[37]

Praxis, therefore, lies at the very heart and centre of liberation theology. Praxis is the basis and prior point of departure for theology. Praxis in the light of the gospel becomes a radical commitment to the cause of the poor or, as it is often referred to 'a preferential option for the poor' as the locus of God's presence in the world and our encounter with Christ. This Christian option for the poor brings about a radical questioning of the social order and its ideology. It denounces all ideological interpretations of poverty. The option for the poor entails a commitment to changing the social system that produced the existing poverty. This in turn creates an obligation to work for the refashioning of a new social order. Poverty is no longer just a matter of fated historical fact. It is now quite clear that the existing social orders that have thrown up so much poverty are by no means fixed or irreformable. Thus the option for the poor goes beyond the summons to individual acts of generosity. As Gutiérrez points out: 'Individual almsgiving and social reformism is a type of love that never leaves its own front porch.'[38] Further, this option for the poor also calls for a new understanding of politics, an understanding which realises that every area of life and human activity has political dimensions to it. Most of all this option for the poor requires a process of enabling the poor themselves to become free and responsible subjects of their own destiny which is one of the basic goals of liberation theology.

Another characteristic of the Christian praxis of opting for the poor is that this particular praxis takes on a conflictive character that cannot be simply brushed aside. This means realising the sometimes uncomfortable truth that there cannot be peace without justice. For too long the commandment of love has been confused with the creation of fictitious harmony. What the gospel says however is that we are to love our enemies and that such love will inevitably involve some conflict between various social classes.[39]

In addition to this fundamental option for the poor, the praxis of liberation opens up a whole new perspective on our understanding of what constitutes knowledge and truth. In fact it points the way to the emergence of a new epistemology, a theme we will have more to say about in chapter three. As Gutiérrez points out it involves:

> breaking with the old ways of thinking and knowing . . .

> and recognising that a great change has taken place in the way people come to know truth and relate it to their practice in history.[40]

This new way of knowing the truth is bound up inextricably with the experience of the praxis of liberation. The praxis of liberation becomes the key to knowledge and truth:

> Knowledge is bound up with transformation. We come to know history . . . in the process of transforming it and ourselves. As Vico put it long ago, we really know only what we ourselves do.[41]

This praxis of liberation that brings about the transformation of life and history is not just the embodiment of some finely worked out 'pure theory'. Rather, the praxis of liberation 'is the matrix of all authentic knowledge' and the source of 'a new kind of discourse about the faith . . . and Christian community'.[42]

In the context of this new perception of knowledge and

truth as linked to the praxis of liberation, Gutiérrez goes on to note that truth in the gospel is primarily something that is to be done. He observes how we are exhorted by John the Evangelist not just to know the truth but 'to do' the truth and that this truth is love. At the same time, however, he is quick to point out that he is not suggesting that there is some mechanical correspondence between the gospel vision of truth and our present-day awareness of the intrinsic relationship that exists between knowing reality and transforming the world. He does, however, wish to draw attention to this new point of convergence in which theological reflection can be framed.[43]

A further characteristic of the praxis of liberation is that it functions as an important 'mediating factor' in communicating the mystery hidden from eternity and now revealed in Christ Jesus: the mystery of the Father's love for his people, the call of all to unity in Christ and the gift of salvation in the Spirit. This divine gift is available only in and through the human realities of community, history, people, and politics. We cannot bypass these mediating factors and move into some realm of the purely sacred. Gutiérrez explicitly denies that this involves any facile equation or reductionism of the sacred to the secular. Instead, he wants to bring out the close relationship that can and does exist between the praxis of liberation in all its different forms and the gift of salvation.[44] Liberation theology differs from other forms of theology in virtue of its peculiar and specific emphasis on liberation praxis. Liberation praxis is the basic point of departure; liberation praxis is the ground, source and context of theological reflection; liberation praxis is the particular perspective we bring to bear on a new reading of the gospel message; liberation praxis is the standpoint from which we ponder the meaning and demands of Christian faith. Further, Gutiérrez wishes to dissociate liberation from those theologies that simply add a tinge of 'social concern' or merely annex the language of liberation to old pastoral and theological postures. In particular Gutiérrez wishes to distinguish liberation theology with its emphasis on praxis and concern for the non-person from most forms of theology done in the Western world. The major point of difference between liberation theology and theology of the West is to be found in the 'objects' of their concern. For liberation theology the primary concern is the 'non-person' at the practical level whereas Western theology has been principally concerned with the 'non-believer' at the theoretical level. The response of liberation theology is one that exists in terms of a praxis for freedom whereas the response of Western theology is one that exists at the level of a theoretical resolution and an intellectual argument.[45]

An Initial Assessment of Liberation Theology

An adequate assessment of liberation theology is clearly beyond the scope of this chapter. However, some initial remarks about its emphasis on the praxis of liberation theology is in order. David Tracy's statement that 'the theological landscape has been changed irretrievably' by liberation theology can hardly be questioned.[46] Liberation theology has given a practical as distinct from a purely theoretical orientation to the Christian faith that was not always visible in the recent past. Further, it has and is providing a powerful Christian witness and counterforce in situations of extreme injustice in the world today. In addition it has overcome the tendency towards individualism, privatisation, and apoliticism that characterised Christian faith so much in the early half of this century.

In particular its emphasis on the centrality of praxis, and all that this implies, is an important corrective to those theoretical strands in Western theology that gave rise to unrestrained idealism and transcendentalism, and the suspicion of ideology which these tend to generate. Probably its most significant contribution has been the recovery of the soteriological motif as central to the entire theological enterprise, a motif that has been smothered in theology for too long. In doing this, Latin American theology, with its emphasis on the praxis of liberation, has made it possible to talk credibly once again about redemption. This does not mean, as Gutiérrez points out again and again to those who persist in distorting the objectives of liberation theology, that liberation is salvation or that salvation is now to be identified with liberation.[47] A further point in favour of liberation theology is its manifest success to date. Here one is reminded of an earlier movement in the history of religion of which it was once said 'if it is of God, it will last'. Liberation theology has overcome not a few attempts at assassination. In its extraordinary capacity to survive it has provided an important paradigm for other legitimate forms of theology concerned with issues of injustice in our world today, such as Black theology and feminist theology. In this regard it should not be forgotten that at present liberation theology is invigorating continents of people (Asia, Africa and Latin America) in the pursuit of justice and peace at a time when the Western world is experiencing a serious malaise in the practice of religious faith.

Probably the most serious challenge to date issued against liberation theology comes from Schubert Ogden. It should be said immediately that Ogden is a sympathetic critic of liberation theology who has as much to say in its favour as he has to say in criticism of it. In general terms it should be noted that Ogden is concerned about the formal as distinct from material characteristics of liberation theology. His criticisms can be reduced to two major areas: liberation theology as a type[48] and the absence of conceptual coherence within liberation theology.[49] Ogden argues against the claim that liberation theology provides a type that is adequate for understanding all Christian theology. Of course, whether liberation theology ever set out to provide a type for understanding all theology is a matter that could and should be at least questioned. It seems more true to say that liberation theology grew as a response to a particular, historical experience specific to the Latin-American continent. To evaluate it as a type for understanding theology may well amount to evaluating that which has only subsequently emerged as a possibility that was not originally envisaged or intended.

Ogden's critique of liberation theology as a type is complex and by no means easy to follow. He points out that liberation theology operates out of a prior commitment to the praxis of liberation but wonders whether this commitment is sufficient to ask and answer the ultimate question of the meaning and truth of Christian witness. Further, he points out that liberation theology seems to rest upon a mistake, that of confusing a contingent connection for a necessary one.[50] By this he seems to mean that on the one hand the presence of much human oppression is contingent whereas the search for the meaning and truth of Christian witness is necessary and intrinsic to Christian theology. In addition, Ogden argues that there has been a further confusion between theology as critical reflection on the Christian witness and theology undertaken as a Christian vocation.[51]

In contrast Ogden understands theology as a process and product of a certain kind of critical reflection. As a process it is concerned with the two-fold question of the meaning and truth of the Christian witness of faith. As a product, it is concerned with a reasoned answer to the question about the meaning and truth of the Christian witness. As both process and product, theology is involved with the ultimate question of the meaning and truth of human existence. This latter constitutes the basic commitment of the theologian.[52]

If we understand Ogden properly here the bone of contention seems to centre around his emphasis on the centrality of the ultimate question about the meaning and truth of existence as foundational to theology, whereas liberation theology's commitment to the praxis of liberation is put forward as central to the theological task. Are these two foundational concerns all that different and all that far apart? The ultimate question about the meaning and truth of existence is itself one particular way of formulating the soteriological question which must surely be central to all theology. Equally, commitment to the praxis of liberation is another way of responding to and formulating the soteriological concern intrinsic to all theology. Are the concerns of liberation theology as directed to the praxis of liberation and

Ogden's understanding of theology as concerned about the meaning and truth of existence all that different? Is there not an underlying unity or at least a relationship between these two preoccupations of all theology?

Furthermore, it should be pointed out that Ogden's distinction between a commitment to the meaning and truth of human existence as reflected in the Christian witness and liberation theology's emphasis on the praxis of freedom is a distinction about elements that should not be separated from each other extrinsically. It is not true to say that the intention of liberation theology is to suggest that the meaning and truth of human existence is only available in and through the praxis of liberation. In addition it must be noted that liberation theology would not go along with Ogden's suggestion that present-day oppression is something that is simply contingent as if one day life could be otherwise. Liberation theology would hold that such oppression is part of the wider reality of sin that reigns in the world which can be reduced in the light of the Gospel though never fully overcome in this life.

Lastly, liberation theology would not accept Ogden's distinction between theology as critical reflection and theology as vocation. Liberation theology clearly rejects the possibility of making such a distinction. While Ogden explicitly acknowledges this claim of liberation theology, he does not accept it. In contrast, liberation theology, supported by political theology, maintains that theological reflection must be earthed in praxis which acts as a check, control and criterion on such reflection. It is by no means clear that Ogden has fully adverted to the radical shift taken by liberation and political theology in according primacy to the praxis of Christian faith.

Ogden argues that what makes one a theologian is not the commitment of faith which one shares as a believing Christian but rather the commitment to ask reflectively and to answer questions about the meaning and truth of existence as expressed in the Christian witness.[53] In other words, Ogden does not accept the claim of liberation theology that if one's work as a theologian is to be concrete and scientific it must be involved in the praxis of liberation.

The second area of major criticism by Ogden concerns the conceptual aspects of liberation theology. According to Ogden, liberation theologians tend 'to focus on the existential meaning of God for us without dealing at all adequately with the metaphysical being of God in himself'.[54] The point at issue here is that Ogden claims that liberation theology fails to take account of the metaphysical implications of a praxis-grounded theology. As a result liberation theology often assumes traditional metaphysical beliefs about God that are uncritical and sometimes even out-of-joint with an emphasis on the primacy of praxis.

Ogden's criticism of the conceptual dimensions of liberation theology should be taken seriously. He has put his finger on a weakness in liberation theology or, to put it perhaps more accurately, on an area that is formally undeveloped in most liberation theologies and therefore in need of critical attention. If God is active in the liberation of humanity and especially the poor, then this has implications for the way we understand and conceive the reality of God. By and large, liberation theology has not worked out metaphysical principles consistent with its mode of theologising. This criticism by Ogden is all the more significant and suggestive when we bear in mind that his own metaphysical position is informed by the tradition of process philosophy.

Some kind of critical interplay between praxis and process at the philosophical and theological level seems called for to meet the difficulties raised by Ogden. Furthermore, if praxis is to succeed then there must be some grasp of the historical process that needs to be changed. Questions about the nature of reality are unavoidable in any serious attempt to alter the social and political *status quo*. Indeed, the way we see the world influences our whole approach to the possibility of creating a new social order and our understanding of the coming of God's Kingdom. Some form of process philosophy with its strong emphasis on the organic character of all existence would seem to provide, from a conceptual and practical point of view, the most adequate and appropriate framework presently available for liberation theology. At the same time a theology of praxis has much to offer to a philosophy of process by way of modification and correction. We shall take up this point about the interplay that might take place between social praxis and process philosophy later on in chapter four.

The value of Ogden's twofold criticism is that it is a timely warning against any attempt by liberation theology to play down the importance of hard-nosed, critical and intellectual rigour in the exercise of theology. Ogden is right in emphasising that theology, especially liberation theology, must not give the impression of 'a soft sell' when it comes to the demands of intellectual reflection and conceptual clarity. At the same time liberation theology is right in insisting that this critical reflection must be tied to and rooted in the praxis of Christian faith. It must be acknowledged that Ogden, while critical of liberation theology, is particularly sensitive to and appreciative of the general direction that Latin-American theology has given theology in general.

By way of conclusion we wish to return to the concerns with which this chapter set out, namely the apparent ineffectiveness of the Christian message in the public forum and the social domain because of what seems to be its highly theoretical character. The turn to praxis as witnessed by political and liberation theology is a forceful corrective to an approach to the meaning of the Christian faith that is too theoretical. The turn to praxis highlights not only the active involvement of theology with things of this world as a necessary point of contact with the transcendent but also points up the critical contribution that Christianity can make out of its gospel vision to the social and political process of contributing to the construction of a better world. The turn to praxis recognises once and for all that religion is ultimately a highly practical matter affecting the way we live and experience social existence. Most of all, this rediscovery of the primacy of praxis requires that critical attention be given to the experience of pastoral practice as a genuine source in theology, while the necessary influence of theology upon this pastoral practice has to be acknowledged. If this can be done, the serious gap that presently exists between theory and practice, personal faith and social experience, life and religion may be significantly reduced.

Two conclusions can be drawn from this analysis of the turn to praxis in contemporary theology. In the first place we wish to suggest that theology is not simply concerned about purely theoretical issues that have little or no bearing on the social and political aspects of human existence. To the contrary, theology is a science grounded in praxis. It is concerned about the intellectual credibility of a particular praxis of Christian faith, hope and love, directed to the creation of a better world in the name of the kingdom of God announced by Jesus Christ. The real contribution of both political and liberation theology is to point up this primacy and centrality of praxis in the performance of theology. Secondly, we wish to propose that this praxis understanding of Christian faith is by no means something new within the authentic Christian tradition. The general orientation of both political and liberation theology is not the proposal of something new but the recovery of an older way of 'doing' theology which was in fact quite characteristic of the early Church. Theology within infant Christianity was directed towards the promotion of a particular way of living, based on and derived from a practical following of the person of Jesus Christ. Theology was about giving a reasonable account of the praxis of faith that would advance the kingdom of God. This return to the spirit of early Christianity is something that is explicitly acknowledged by political and liberation theology. Metz points out:

> Christianity as a community of those who believe in Jesus Christ has, from the very beginning not been primarily a community interpreting and arguing but a community remembering ... with a practical intention — a ... memory of the passion, death and resurrection of Jesus. Faith ... can ... be translated into dangerously liberating stories, the hearer who is affected by them becoming not simply a hearer, but a doer of the word.[55]

In a similar and equally significant tone liberation theology claims:

We know . . . that for Christ and for the primitive Church the essential element did not consist in the reduction of the message . . . to systematic categories of intellectual comprehension but in creating new habits of acting and living in the world.[56]

2

Praxis and its Philosophical Background

In recent times, especially since the Second Vatican Council, it could be said that theology has taken to the streets. An urgent concern with questions about action for human rights and social justice has moved to the centre of the theological stage. Indeed, the possibility of a purely academic theology — that is, a theology which engages in reflection without reference to the concrete, historical and social circumstances of humanity — is now a matter of some debate. This development is yet another manifestation of the turning towards praxis in theology which we have been examining in chapter one. One of the many striking features about this turning towards praxis in theology is that it seems to have taken place more or less simultaneously in quite different parts of the world. This fact alone is enough to suggest that the move to praxis is of major importance to the Christian community.

An explicit concern with praxis can be found, as we have already seen, in the political theologies coming out of Europe in the late sixties and early seventies. This is apparent not only in the writings of J.B. Metz but also among other theologians. For example J. Moltmann points out that the 'freedom of faith ... urges men on towards liberating actions, because it makes them painfully aware of suffering in situations of exploitation, oppression, alienation and captivity ...'.[1] Around the same time, some will want to argue a few years later, we had the development of liberation theology in Latin America. Over and above Gutiérrez we find other Latin American theologians focusing on the primacy of praxis. For instance H. Assman talks about 'the importance of practice as a starting point for the theology of liberation . . . in which the task of transforming the world is . . . intimately linked to the interpretation of the world'.[2] These two distinct theologies[3] in turn gave rise at a later stage in North America to the construction of what some call 'practical theology'[4] and others refer to as 'critical theology',[5] both of which are still finding their own specific identity. In broad terms, practical theology may be said to address the needs of society via a praxis that seeks to transform those structures which shape the quality of social existence. Critical theology, again in general terms, is concerned about putting its own house in order by examining the underlying presuppositions of theology and submitting these to an ideology-critique before turning to the needs of society.

The meaning, place and role of praxis in theology is of primary concern in these different styles of theology today. Some see the question of praxis as one method in theology. Others see it as an issue affecting specific areas of theology in a radical way, such as Christology and ecclesiology. Lonergan remarks, somewhat enigmatically, that it is only after the age of innocence has passed that praxis becomes a serious academic issue.[6] Matthew Lamb holds that the issue of praxis is *the* key question in theology today.[7]

The purpose of this chapter is to examine the philosophical lineage of the concept of praxis. This will involve a historical survey of the place of praxis in philosophy, an outline of Marx's understanding of praxis, and finally the role of praxis among the critical theorists of Frankfurt.

From Aristotle to Marx

The first point to note about the concept of praxis is the preference by many commentators for the Greek usage of the word. This preference is quite deliberate. It alerts us to the fact that the English word 'practice' does not capture or adequately translate the subtleties implied in the Greek usage. For one thing 'praxis' does not imply simply the application of theory to practice. Further, praxis does not exist free floating in isolation as it were from theory or in contrast to it. These particular nuances within the term 'praxis' can only be fully appreciated by looking at the history of this complex concept from Aristotle through Marx to the twentieth-century critical theorists.

According to Aristotle there are three kinds of knowledge which are designated by the terms *theoria, praxis* and *poiesis*, corresponding more or less to three kinds of living that we may call the contemplative life (philosophical), the practical life (political) and the productive life (survival activity). *Theoria* is directed to the life of contemplation. It carries with it some religious connotation insofar as it implies going into the temple to reflect on the eternal verities or at least some form of withdrawal from the hurly-burly of daily life in order to find the truth. As such the life of reflection was regarded by Aristotle as an end in itself. *Praxis*, on the other hand, is concerned with the personal participation of the individual in the life of the *polis*. More specifically praxis is directed to the right ordering of human behaviour in the socio-political world. Praxis, in contrast to the speculative reason of *theoria*, operates out of practical reason. Praxis is about reflective ethical action which is exercised in a political context; it is always a purposeful activity; it is action inspired by reflection and reflection animated by action. *Poiesis*, the third form of human activity, is a process of making those things which are necessary for the survival of human beings. *Poiesis* is about production: it is the exercise of technical skills by different people; it is the creation of artifacts; it is a process of human making.[8]

By and large Aristotle extols the life of contemplation. *Theoria* is an end in itself and is held up as an ideal which should be supported by *poiesis* and *praxis*. At the same time, however, it is not altogether true to say that Aristotle separates *theoria* and *praxis*. If anything, he wishes to overcome the Platonic idea of pure philosophy devoid from life. Indeed for Aristotle the good politician cannot avoid being a philosopher and vice versa. After all the philosopher is also a human being who must live out his life in the *polis* even though he may be searching for that which transcends the contingency of the political order. Furthermore, Aristotle does point out that we do not simply wish to know what virtue (justice) is but, we also wish to be virtuous (just).[9]

Thus one might say that there is a unity and interplay between *poiesis, praxis* and *theoria*, and in that particular order. Rather than oppose *praxis* and *theoria*, Aristotle wanted to keep politics and philosophy, the practical life and the contemplative life, together.

It is extremely difficult to charter the contours of the philosophical debate after Aristotle in regard to the relation between *theoria* and praxis without going into details beyond the purpose of this chapter. However, a broad generalisation (with some exceptions) would be that over the centuries there was a move towards the primacy of the contemplative life which downgraded the political life. In the early Christian centuries, most of the Greek fathers of the Church would have subscribed to Origen's statement that 'the active life is the stirrup to contemplation'.[10] This general tendency was reinforced by the speculative and intellectual orientation of Greek philosophy. A strongly rational and theoretical bent became part and parcel of Christian theology. A notable exception to this broad sweep — and some few others could also be cited — can be found in Augustine, who echoes Aristotle, in *The City of God*. There Augustine points out that there are:

... three modes of life, the contemplative, the active, the contemplative-active. A man can live the life of faith in any of these three and get to heaven ... no man must be so committed to contemplation as ... to give no thought to his neighbour's needs, nor so absorbed in action as to dispense with the contemplation of God.[11]

Clearly Augustine favours the contemplative-active life or what Aristotle called praxis. In the centuries after Augustine through the Middle Ages 'no Latin author before Duns Scotus (1265–1308) ever used the expression 'praxis' in a philosophical or theological context'.[12] Scotus, as another exception, poses the question: *Quid sit praxis?* He sees praxis as something that succeeds the intellect, that which we would call today an act of the will. His intention is to show that 'theology is a *practica cognitio* in the sense that it precedes and prepares a love of God ... the culminating

point of all theological theorising.'[13] More particularly,
Scotus states 'that God is the 'doable knowable' (*cognoscibile
operabile*), that is the object of knowledge which may be
reached by a doing which is true praxis'.[14] However, the
insights of Scotus could hardly be said to have won out. To
the contrary, a concern for contemplative knowledge and
theoretical reason continued down through the centuries to
the eighteenth century. The primacy of theory, with some
notable exceptions, dominated theology.

It is extremely difficult to label accurately the philosophical revolution that took place in the period of the
Enlightenment. One possible way, suggested by Richard J.
Bernstein is his important work *Praxis and Action*, is to note
the anthropological shift that took place in the move from
the individual as Knower to the individual as Agent.[15] This
understanding of the person as knower was based on 'an
incorrigibly contemplative conception of knowledge'.[16] The
move to the person as agent was facilitated by a variety of
factors. The discoveries of science in the eighteenth century
opened up new possibilities for humanity in terms of making,
unmaking and remaking the world. A new confidence in the
creative power of reason and the promise of science was
dawning. This new enthusiasm is reflected in Kant's critique
of pure reason and his avowed preference for practical
reason. In this preference Kant effected a move towards the
individual as subject in a way that highlighted the autonomy
of the individual self. The human person is no longer determined simply by a given cosmic order. Instead the individual
as subject constructs his or her own world. However, the
problem with Kant was his failure to grapple with the social
and historical conditions of human existence and to apply
the importance of the turning towards the subject to the
socio-political world. This failure of Kant undoubtedly
influenced the works of Hegel and Marx significantly.

Marx, via Hegel, on Praxis

With Hegel and Marx the technical concept of *praxis* returns
to the centre of the philosophical debate. Our remarks on
Hegel will be restricted simply to the provision of a point of

entry into the philosophy of Marx.

At the centre of Hegel's complex system we have the concept of Absolute Spirit (*Geist*). Spirit, for Hegel, is the guiding principle of history and everything in the world is related to Spirit. Spirit is that dynamic, dialectical and absolute process of becoming which develops the universe by actualising itself in history. This all-pervasive and all-determining Spirit in history is guided ultimately by Divine Providence. It is the individual who reflects the development of Spirit. The individual is the agent through which the Spirit expresses itself in history. Thus it is Hegel's understanding of the individual that gives us access to the absolute principle of Spirit. Hegel says of the individual: 'Man is his own action, the sequence of his actions, that into which he has been making himself.'[17] This in turn is reflected in Hegel's description of Spirit: 'The very essence of Spirit is action. It makes itself what it essentially is; it is its own product, its own work.'[18] It is this particular understanding of the individual and Spirit in Hegel that was to have a profound influence on Marx.[19] As such this perspective of Hegel constituted a major step in the gradual movement from the individual as knower to the individual as agent. It also paved the way, indirectly, for establishing the primacy of praxis in philosophy over against the control of theory.

It should be remembered that Spirit, for Hegel, is always in a continuous state of conflict, 'is at war with itself'.[20] Thus Spirit seeks to overcome these contradictions through dialectical activity: affirmation, critical negation and forward movement (*aufgehoden*). This dynamic process of resolving conflict 'is mediated through consciousness'.[21] Once again it is by looking at the nature of self-consciousness that we can best understand this dynamic activity of Spirit in the world. Self-consciousness comes into being through contact with other selves and it is a similar kind of process that spurs the activity of the world Spirit forward in history

It is within the context of this all-encompassing activity of Spirit in the world, evolving towards freedom, that we can situate Hegel's understanding of praxis. Praxis, for Hegel, is the praxis of Spirit realising itself in history. The rational element in this praxis of Spirit is that which constitutes consciousness. Our consciousness of this rational moment in the praxis of Spirit is what makes up theory. Hegel once said 'theory rises only at sundown': it comes after the praxis of Spirit in history; it is the expression of the rational element in the praxis of Spirit. Praxis, then, is the unfolding activity of the Spirit in the world and theory is the rational articulation of that praxis. There is a unity between praxis and theory for Hegel. It should be noted that this unity between praxis and theory is a unity between the praxis of Spirit and the theory proposed by the individual. Theory, human knowledge, is always about the praxis of Spirit and not the praxis of the individual person in the world. It was this understanding of praxis and theory in Hegel that provoked Marx into developing his own particular view of the theory-praxis relationship.

It is against this sketchy background on Hegel that we can now look at Marx's basic philosophy of praxis. Marx came to Hegel via the so-called Young Hegelians who sensed many of the things that Marx would later develop. Marx from the very beginning 'felt deeply that there was something essentially right and something desperately wrong with Hegelianism'.[22] He was both fascinated by the grand synthesis of Hegel and appalled by its inability to change the world.

One of the major criticisms by Marx of Hegel concerns the question of praxis. He found Hegel's understanding of praxis far too idealistic and ultimately ideological. Hegel's idea of praxis as the praxis of Spirit did nothing to change the course of history, or to bring about freedom in the world. In making this criticism Marx does give Hegel credit for recognising the importance of praxis. At the same time, however, Marx wants to replace the praxis of Spirit with the praxis of humanity. In other words, Marx sets out 'to anthropologise' Hegel's grand synthesis, to replace the praxis of Spirit by a praxis of human beings. The subject of world history is not Spirit guided by Providence but the praxis of individual human beings.

Having stood Hegel on his head, Marx develops his own peculiar and complex philosophy of praxis. Part of the problem in unravelling Marx's understanding of praxis is that it belongs to a larger complexity within his writings. This larger complexity consists of the existence within Marx of two apparently contradictory streams running alongside each other throughout his works. These two streams have been recognised by most commentators in recent times and have been brought to the fore with particular clarity by Alvin Gouldner in his important work *The Two Marxisms: Contradiction and Anomalies in the Development of Theory*. These two streams are now referred to by most authors as Scientific Marxism and Critical Marxism.

The scientific stream is that part of Marx's thought which deals with the given structures of capitalist society. These structures are governed according to Marx by blind and necessary laws which, though they presently maintain the capitalist mode of production in existence, will eventually lead to a classless society. This particular stream in Marx gives rise to certain forms of materialism and determinism. Alongside this scientific stream there also exists the critical Marx. This is the side of Marx which is concerned with changing the given structures of the social and political world in which we live out our lives. This change can be brought about by effecting a creative praxis. This particular stream corresponds to the political and voluntarist elements of Marxist thought.

Unfortunately these two streams are portrayed by some, including Gouldner in his otherwise impressive book, as an unwitting contradiction within Marxist thought. For Gouldner the two Marxisms undermine each other. A more informed reading of Marx however would suggest that these two streams are in fact interrelated, dialectically complementary, and ultimately self-generating. In other words, it is precisely Marx's acute awareness of the given structures of society that drives him to posit the need for radical change. The 'two Marxisms' do not necessarily contradict, cancel, or oppose each other. To the contrary, Marx's 'preoccupation with the identification and depiction of limits, structures, "laws", the "realm of necessity", must be seen not as an unacknowledged refutation of his commitment to the promise of human agency in history but rather as an essential part of that very commitment'.[23]

It is within the context of this larger complexity in Marx's thought that we must situate his philosophy of praxis. As Gouldner helpfully points out, these two streams in Marx have given rise to two particular perceptions of praxis.[24] On the one hand there is the blind praxis of unreflective labour which is necessary to keep the institutions of the capitalist world in existence. This praxis, as we shall presently see, is the source of alienation within society. On the other hand there is the creative praxis that is directed towards changing the social conditions of the working masses and whose basic aim is emancipation. One might talk therefore about the blind praxis of the scientific Marx and the creative praxis of the critical Marx. While it is the latter which is our primary concern here, namely the creative praxis of the critical Marx, we must remember that it is only available to us in reference to the blind praxis of the scientific, materialist Marx.

The real problem with human existence for Marx is that the systems which people have created through blind praxis are the source of human alienation. This praxis gives rise to production but once the individual is separated from the products of his or her praxis then these 'objectifications' become the source of alienation. The point Marx is making here about alienation does not derive simply from the fact that the products of human praxis as 'objects' are simply extrinsic to the agent of praxis and therefore alien. Rather, his theory of alienation is based on his radically anthropological understanding of praxis. Just as Hegel had pointed out that the self is what it does, so Marx now takes up that principle and brings it a step further to include also the products of praxis. For Marx, the individual is what he or she does: the nature and character of the individual is determined (intrinsically) by praxis. The human person is shaped by praxis. At the same time, however, Marx also wants to say that the products of praxis embody some aspects of the individual; the individual puts something of himself or herself into his or her world and product. Not all 'objectifications' of praxis necessarily result in alienation. After all 'objectifications' are necessary for material existence. Rather, alienation occurs when the products of one's own praxis are taken over by others and made into objects of exchange without reference to their original source. When this happens the 'objects' of praxis begin to master, control and dehumanise the person's praxis in a way that produces alienation. Thus certain forms of praxis, namely the capitalistic mode of production, give rise to alienation. Marx sums up this process as it takes place in capitalistic society in the following terms:

> The realization of labor is its objectification. In the viewpoint of political economy this realization of labor appears as the diminution of the worker, the objectification of the loss of and subservience to the object, and the appropriation as alienation, as externalization.[25]

Marx reacts further against the idealism of Hegel by subordinating consciousness to praxis and social existence: 'The production of ideas, of conception, of consciousness is directly interwoven with the material activity and material relationships of men . . . consciousness does not determine life, but life determines consciousness.'[26] It is this principle of praxis determining consciousness that is the basis of Marx's scientific materialism. Historical materialism in Marx implies that the material conditions of life, especially the historical mode of producing the material means of existence, determines the shape of human consciousness; theory is the expression and articulation of consciousness based on the material conditions resulting from praxis.

On the other hand Marx, that is, the critical Marx in contrast to the scientific Marx, is quite adamant in his writings that praxis must be informed by some critical understanding of the social situations. Praxis must never be merely a blind uncritical praxis. Further, the theory that informs praxis must be a theory that both understands and criticises the existing social conditions. Marx's primary concern is directed to a diagnosis of present social circumstances. As such he has little time for speculating about the future. The only way to change the world is to diagnose the present circumstances via a 'relentless criticism of all existing conditions . . . not afraid of its findings and just as little afraid of the conflict'.[27] Criticism, relentless criticism, is a central category in Marx's system and the purpose of such criticism is the transformation of social reality. Such criticism is efficacious only when it enables people to bring to self-consciousness the reasons why they are suffering and alienated and what they can do to change the causes of such suffering and alienation. It was the combination of critical understanding and human activity that provided the basis for Marx's (in)famous concept of 'revolutionary praxis' (= practical critical activity). It is at this second critical level that Marx makes a most significant contribution to a philosophy of praxis. Praxis must be informed by a critical understanding of social reality. At the same time this critical understanding must be in touch with the blind praxis taking place at ground level.

One way of drawing together these ideas of Marx on praxis is to go back to some of his eleven 'theses' on Feuerbach.[28] Although these were written in 1845 by Marx when he was twenty-seven years old and only published posthumously, they were in many respects programmatic for his subsequent work. Certainly the most basic thesis is the eleventh which states: 'The philosophers have only interpreted the world; the point is to change it.' This sums up Marx's programme and helps us to understand the primary place he gives to critical praxis. The role of praxis in unity with a critical understanding of social reality is to change the world. This concern with changing the world is also found in thesis three which points out:

> The materialistic doctrine concerning the change of circumstances and education forgets that circumstances are changed by men . . . the coincidence of the change of circumstances and of human activity or self change can be comprehended . . . only as revolutionary praxis.

Change, for Marx, comes through praxis and not from ideas about materialistic doctrine. There is nothing predetermined about the social and historical circumstances of life. Marx, in contrast to the fashionable streams of positivism and empiricism in the twentieth century, was far from impressed or taken in by 'the myth of the given'. Further, the change which comes through praxis is by no means unrelated to questions about knowledge and truth. These latter are touched upon in Marx's second thesis on Feuerbach: 'The question whether human thinking can reach objective truth — is not a question of theory but a practical question . . . the dispute about the actuality or non-actuality of thinking — thinking isolated from practice — is a purely scholastic question.' Here Marx is proposing in-embryo basic orientations for a new epistemology. Knowledge is primarily a practical issue; it is something which originates in praxis. Knowledge, therefore, is not to be found only in the contemplation of 'things the way they actually are'. Consequently, truth cannot be understood simply as some kind of correspondence between the mind and reality. Instead truth is a practical issue, available to us in praxis. When this particular thesis is tied up with Marx's view on alienation we begin to see how little time he has for the 'is-ought', 'descriptive-prescriptive' dichotomies of human understanding.

Whatever way we approach Marx we continually come back to the basic idea of critical and creative praxis. Indeed, this particular praxis is the master concept throughout Marx's writings.[29] We have seen that praxis is a multi-layered concept embracing in varying degrees relentless criticism, human activity, historical change, labour/production, and alienation.

The Critical Theorists of Frankfurt

These ideas of Marx, and many others which have not been touched upon here, have spawned different movements in the history of social and political thought. One such movement is that which has come to be known as Critical Theory, associated with the Frankfurt School in Germany. This movement began with a small group of intellectuals in 1923 who set up an Institute for Social Research in Frankfurt. They were forced to move to the United States in the thirties and returned subsequently in the late forties. They came to prominence in the late fifties and mid-sixties especially. The founding fathers of this new school of critical thought were Max Horkheimer, Theodoro Adorno and Herbert Marcuse.

Jürgen Habermas could be described as a second-generation critical theorist.

Critical theory is important because it advances, better than any other group, Marx's radical ideas about praxis and critique. Critical theory is significant because if offers a rigorous analysis of contemporary society, science and culture at a time when there is a growing awareness that something serious is wrong about the direction of the western world. It is also noteworthy because it has influenced and continues to influence political, liberation, practical, and critical theology.[30]

Critical theory came into being as a kind of 'intellectual resistance to the mechanisation of Marxism in theory and practice'.[31] On the one hand, the ideal of the theorist as a disinterested observer was gaining ground in the early twentieth century. A new kind of positivism was becoming popular under the influence of the so-called scientific method. A value-free scientism in social theory was influencing many forms of human living. An objectivism, the reification of the intellectual disciplines, was becoming more and more acceptable. Practice was being reduced simply to the technical application of theoretical knowledge. And in particular, practice seemed to be innocent of any critical import and ethical content. Most of all the intrinsic critical unity between theory and praxis that Marx had worked so hard to achieve was being sundered once and for all. A clear dichotomy between fact and value, is and ought, the descriptive and prescriptive, ruled the day. On the other hand within the philosophies of life there was a turn towards subjectivity and interiority, a neglect of the materialist conditions of human existence, and a forgetfulness of the importance of action in the historical world.[32] Critical theory was an attempt to halt this creeping mechanisation of life and the turn towards individualism by recovering some of the basic principles of Marx while at the same time being prepared to go beyond these principles.

The best point of entry into critical theory is to be found in M. Horkheimer's programmatic paper 'Traditional and Critical Theory.'[33] In this important essay Horkheimer outlines the meaning of critical theory by contrasting it with traditional theory.

Traditional theory, as perceived by Horkheimer, sets out to formulate basic principles and objective knowledge which can become regulative for natural sciences. The goal of traditional theory 'is a universal systematic science . . . the same conceptual apparatus . . . elaborated for . . . inanimate nature is serving . . . animate nature as well. . .'.[34] Traditional theory attempts to present 'pure knowledge', which is separate from and independent of human action. Thus there is something of a split in the life of the individual who is a traditional theorist:

> The scholarly specialist 'as' scientist regards social reality . . . as extrinsic to him, and 'as' citizen exercises his interest . . . through political articles, membership in political parties. . . . But he does not unify these two activities. . .[35]

By way of reaction critical theory denies that it is possible or legitimate to construct a system of universal applicability and sees this desire as a dangerous form of positivism with more than a tendency towards support for the status quo. Further, critical theory, Horkheimer argues, refuses to make a fetish out of knowledge as something separate from and superior to human action. In addition, the suggestion that the specialist can work in a totally detached manner living in a society in which he or she is not yet autonomous is untenable.

One of the central theses of critical theory is the claim that there is a basic and intrinsic connection between knowledge and human interest, a thesis developed at some length by J. Habermas in his book *Knowledge and Interest*. Critical theory openly acknowledges such a connection which, within its own self-understanding, it identifies as a practical interest in improving the quality and character of human existence in the future. Critical theory is always guided by a formal interest in the future. In particular, critical theory is committed to the creation of those conditions whereby 'mankind will for the first time be a conscious subject and actively determine its own way of life'.[36] In this regard the critical theorist sees himself 'as forming a dynamic unity with the oppressed class, so that his presentation of societal contradiction is not merely an expression of concrete historical situations but also a force within it to stimulate change'.[37] Not only does critical theory openly acknowledge its own specific interests but also explicitly declares itself committed to action. Critical theory is quick to point out that the divorce between theory and action so characteristic of traditional theory and the resulting dualism between fact and value that this promotes is basically ideological, serving to promote the status quo. In view of this, critical theory is concerned to raise the awareness level of its subjects to see the contradictions of human existence and to eliminate the different forms of false consciousness maintaining this present perception of social reality. Further in this important paper, Horkheimer argues that the verification of or falsification of the basic truths of critical theory cannot be undertaken by reference to the present social order because they imply the possibility of a different social reality. Elsewhere, in a different article, Horkheimer suggests however that critical theory does have a principle of verification insofar as such exists in practical testing: 'Truth is a moment in correct praxis; he who identifies it with success leaps over history and becomes an apologist for the dominant reality.'[38] Truth, therefore, for critical theory, is a dynamic moment in that particular praxis which changes the social conditions of life. In other words, the verification of theory comes through a relationship with right praxis. Once truth becomes frozen, however, there is a real danger of the present dominating the future. The point to be noted here is that basic to critical theory is the underlying principle that theory guides praxis and praxis is the truth of theory. A dialectic obtains between theory and praxis that generates an ongoing perception of the truth. The circularity of this line of reasoning is not a matter of concern for critical theory provided the dialectic between theory and praxis is really operative. The other major criticism made by critical theory was directed against the town criers of interiority. This tendency towards interiority and withdrawal was in effect an escape from and denial of historical reality. In opposition to this, Adorno pointed out: 'Inwardness is the historical prison of pre-historical humanity.'[39]

It should be noted here that critical theory is by no means a rehash of the teaching of Karl Marx. In many instances it explicitly goes beyond Marx. For example in Marx it is the working class who are to be the agents of social change. Horkheimer, however, claims that circumstances in the twentieth century have changed and that the working class may not necessarily be the best suited for this role. One of the functions of critical theory is to overcome the conformist tendency that can be found among the working classes. Critical theory, therefore, does not see itself simply as the spokesperson of one class but as the ally of all forces prepared to tell the truth.[40] Further, Marx had concentrated his attention on economic matters whereas critical theory widens the discussion by embracing the critiques of Nietzsche and Freud with particular reference to the proliferation of mass culture. In addition, while it is true to say that critical theory accepts the spirit of Marx's critique of political economy it nonetheless questions some of the underlying assumptions of Marx's thesis: that the development of capitalism would give rise to the classless society, the relative neglect of the subjective conditions necessary for the emancipation of the proletariat, the tendency to reduce praxis to instrumental action (*techne*).[41]

Habermas and Praxis

Following the foundational work of Horkheimer and other first-generation critical theorists whom we have not touched upon here, comes the contribution of Jürgen Habermas who advances and in many respects goes beyond the early critical theorists. It would be as foolish as it is impossible to pretend to summarise adequately the enormously complex thinking of Habermas who has been likened to a latter-day Hegel. Our selection of basic themes in Habermas will be limited by our search for further understanding concerning the relationship between theory and praxis.

One of the major concerns of Habermas is an exposition of the confusion that exists in industrially advanced societies between the practical and the technical. A basic characteristic of modern society is the identification of technical reason with practical reason. According to Habermas:

> The relationship of theory to praxis can . . . only assert itself as the purposive — rational application of techniques assured by empirical science. The social potential of science is reduced to the powers of technical control . . . the empirical, analytical sciences produce technical recommendations, but they furnish no answer to practical questions.[42]

Habermas distinguishes between the practical and the technical in much the same way as Aristotle distinguishes between praxis and *techne (poiesis)*. The problem with modern society, which is based on science, technology, industry and administration, is that the distinction between the practical and the technical not only has collapsed but, even worse, the technical domain has usurped the place of the practical: '. . . no attempt . . . is made to attain a rational consensus on the part of citizens with the practical control of their destiny. Its place is taken by the attempt to attain technical control over history. . .'[43] Over and above the demise of concern for the practical that these developments have brought, there is also the additional difficulty that this prevailing technological consciousness has become an ideology with legitimating power. Further, this confusion between the technical and the practical is the logical outcome of the claim that science is value-free. In effect, what has happened is that the empirical sciences in their obsession to be value-free and detached have indeed replaced one scheme of practical values by another scheme of impersonal, technical and instrumental values.

It is precisely this problem of *techne* taking over from praxis that Habermas tackles in his book *Knowledge and Human Interest*. He describes the process that gave rise to this positivistic state of affairs as 'the disillusion of epistemology', and the challenge as one of recovering the 'abandoned stages of reflection',[44] especially critical reflection as put forward by Kant. The basic and distinctive thesis which he puts forward is that *knowledge is guided by interest*. This thesis is proposed in opposition to a disinterested and objectivistic understanding of theory (knowledge) found in classical philosophy and modern positivism. Such philosophy and positivism in different ways assume that knowledge can be arrived at free from 'the natural interests of life and their irritating influence', and both aim at 'describing the universe theoretically in its law-like order, just as it is'.[45] This 'objectivist illusion . . . suppresses the transcendental framework that is the precondition of the meaning of the validity of such propositions' of knowledge.[46] The so-called ideal of 'pure knowledge', theory stripped of all its presuppositions, is as dangerous as it is deceptive.

In contrast to this widespread positivism Habermas suggests that all theory is shaped by the existence of underlying 'cognitive interests'. These interests could be described as basic orientations that influence what counts as the objects and types of knowledge. There are three basic 'cognitive-constitutive interests': the technical, the practical and the emancipatory. These three basic types of knowledge are not arbitrarily chosen. To the contrary the first two, namely the technical and the practical are respectively 'rooted in the specific fundamental conditions of possible reproduction and self constitution of the human species'.[47] The third interest, the emancipatory interest, derives from that basic thrust within the human subject through self-reflection towards autonomy and responsibility. The emancipatory interest in knowledge arises 'out of systematically distorted communication and thinly legitimate repression'.[48] In other words it is the presence of structures of distorted communication that ultimately evoke the emancipatory interest of knowledge.

These three 'knowledge-constitutive interests' are therefore anthropologically grounded in an understanding of what the individual is and can be. They should not be seen as 'influences on cognition that have to be eliminated for the sake of objectivity of knowledge; rather they . . . determine the aspect under which reality can be objectified and . . . made accessible to experience. . .'[49] Habermas assigns these cognitive interests a 'quasi transcendental status'.

Corresponding to each of these three interests are naturally enough three different types of sciences. The technical interest gives rise to the empirical-analytic sciences, the practical to the historical-hermeneutical sciences, and the emancipatory to the socially critical sciences. Each of these sciences in turn is determined by a particular dimension of social existence: 'work, interaction and power'. These different interests, with their corresponding sciences and different aspects of social life are irreducible to one another and yet they are closely interrelated. These orientations towards technical control, a mutual understanding in the conduct of life and emancipation establish a specific point of view from which we approach reality.

At the level of technical interest we have the empirical-analytic sciences which are concerned with the social action of work and relate to issues of human survival. Here the interest is one of technical control over nature through instrumental reason, issuing in purposive-rational action. The principal difficulty Habermas has with this level of knowledge is its pretence to being the only legitimate type of knowledge. For Habermas the technical is merely a part of a larger body of theory and praxis.

The second level of interest is the practical, which gives rise to the historical-hermeneutical sciences and results in the praxis of social interaction. By interaction Habermas means communicative action and intersubjective understanding between human beings made possible by tradition and language. Individuals are shaped not only by work but also by the way they interact with one another at the level of meaning and discourse. Here the historical-hermeneutical sciences help to provide the conditions for reciprocal communication and inter-subjectivity among different individuals and groups by way of unconstrained consensus.[50] Habermas is as critical of those who try to make this level of symbolic interaction between people the only level of knowledge as he is of those who wish to give primacy to technical control.

The main difficulty at this level is that the historical-hermeneutical sciences are too concerned with maintaining mutual understanding within the tradition as it is given. Not enough critical attention is directed to uncovering the distortions that exist within the received tradition. The historical-hermeneutical sciences are not sufficiently self-critical and therefore tend to support the status quo. In effect they fail to realise the emancipatory interest of critical reason. It was this latter criticism that was the subject of an important debate and disagreement between Habermas and Gadamer. For Habermas the problem with hermeneutics is that it approaches the text as isolated from its social context and independent of the particular life praxis that generated the text in the first instance. This eliminates the possibility of critically challenging the tradition of the text.[51]

The third and most basic level of interest is the emancipatory one. This level of cognitive interest is derived from the technical and the practical modes of knowledge. If we examine the knowledge we derive from the technical and the practical we will discover that they are directed towards the creation of the material and intellectual conditions necessary for emancipation. This emancipatory interest gives rise to the critique of ideology and calls for a deeper self-reflection. Habermas likens the procedures of the social sciences interested in emancipation to that of psychoanalysis as introduced by Freud. The therapeutic relationship that exists between the patient and the analyst in psychoanalysis parallels the process that takes place in a critical theory of society. The analyst is not concerned simply to impart information to the patient or simply to apply theory as a remedy. Instead the analyst seeks to enable the patient to overcome the inner resistances maintaining the illness. Success will come not from the analyst's understanding of the patient but from the patient's ability to enter into a deeper self-reflection that will dissolve resistances and thereby effect a transformation. The value of the psycho-analytical model is that it illustrates how the emancipatory interest, either of the individual patient or of the social group, requires a critical analysis of the self-formative processes. From the point of view of society what is needed by the cognitive interests of emancipation is a critique of ideology. An important analogy exists for Habermas between the role of psychoanalysis at the individual level and the role of critical theory in regard to society. Both are concerned to effect an emancipation.

In developing his understanding of emancipation Habermas appeals, with qualification, to Marx's critique of political economy. He disagrees, however, with many aspects of Marx: his exclusive emphasis on a dialectic of labour, his somewhat positivist understanding of critique, his restriction of critique to political economy and the absence in Marx of any epistemological foundation of critique itself. So while he appeals to Marx's critique of ideology and Freud's psychoanalysis as examples of what should take place in the critical inquiry of the social sciences, he is also aware of their limitations.

When pressed to develop this third element of the emancipatory interest, Habermas develops a complex theory of communicative competence. It should be kept in mind that the primary purpose of this theory of communicative action is to clarify the import of the knowledge-constitutive element of emancipation. Habermas sets out to discover a new rationality for understanding this emancipatory interest, a rationality that will critically ground the emancipatory orientation, a rationality that will show that the option for emancipation is more than an existential whim.

In working out his theory of communicative competence Habermas follows more or less the approach of Marx in developing a critique of political economy. For Marx it is only by examining what is, namely the existing forms of alienation, that we discover the historical potentialities of human beings. We can do this because we do not have to accept what is as absolutely given but rather as one historical expression of the potentiality of human existence. In a similar vein Habermas argues that by examining human discourse we can discover the conditions for an ideal speech situation that would result in unrestrained communication and dialogue.

All linguistic communication assumes an underlying consensus among the speakers. This consensus is made up of at least four claims to validity which are accepted by the speakers: 'the comprehensibility of the utterance, the truth of its propositional component, the correctness of its performatory component, and the authenticity of the speaking subject'.[52] A problem arises in communication when this consensus is questioned. Once this happens a distinction arises between the accepted consensus, now in question, and rational discourse as something to be reached. The transition from assumed consensus to rationally determined consensus can only be reached by way of argumentation. But argumentation itself presupposes a consensus of some kind. Habermas is keenly aware of how close he is here to the vicious circle. His solution to this difficulty is found in his thesis that the ideal speech act is both presupposed and anticipated in every speech act. He claims that 'the design of an ideal speech situation is implied in the structure of potential speech since all speech . . . is orientated towards the idea of truth'.[53] The ideal speech situation is directed to the ideas of truth, freedom and justice. As such we cannot realise this ideal but we can anticipate it in our discourse. In other words Habermas holds that implicit in speech acts there is the presence of an ideal speech situation and it is this that is the normative foundation of communication. In ordinary communication there is an assumed consensus. When the validity of the claims in the assumed consensus is questioned we begin to presuppose and anticipate the ingredients of ideal discourse.

An ideal discourse situation exists when there is no other compulsion present than that of fair argumentation, and no form of domination exists among the participants. This conception of ideal speech comes very close, Habermas admits, to Peirce's notion of the ideal community of inquirers. In brief, the ideal speech situation implies the ideal form of social life: freedom from all external and internal constraints where consensus may be reached through the best argument. Habermas sees the ideal speech situation as an anticipation of that form of life in which human autonomy and responsibility are possible.[54]

It might be objected here that Habermas has departed from the underlying issue of the unity that obtains between theory and praxis. The linguistic turn seems to be a far cry from social praxis. Have we arrived at yet another largely theoretical discussion about the dynamics of knowledge which is removed from the social praxis of individuals in society? To react in this way is to misread Habermas and to fall into that understanding of praxis and theory which Habermas is most anxious to eliminate, namely a merely technical appreciation of theory and knowledge awaiting instant application in practice.

Habermas warns us passionately against this simplistic approach to the theory-praxis issue. Theory can never be used simply to justify political action. When this happens there is the assumption that theoretical statements can provide an absolute authority in deciding what is to be done. Even worse, when this happens it is usually a technical understanding of theory that is operative. Such an understanding will destroy the dialectic of theory and praxis. Thus Habermas states explicitly: 'Decisions for the political struggle cannot at the outset be justified theoretically and then carried out organizationally . . . there can be no theory which at the outset can assure a world-historical mission in return for potentional sacrifices.'[55]

Some will see this insistence on the gap between theory and praxis as a failure in Habermas. Those who think this way expect theory to tell us how to change the world. What they fail to recognise is that they are trying to reduce all political action to technical control and instrumental manipulation. They are walking blindfold into that dangerous trap of requesting theory, science in this case, to provide, once and for all, authoritative answers about what is to be done.[56] In doing this they forget that scientism in theory is authoritarianism in practice.[57] The history of our world, especially in the twentieth century, is surely adequate warning against the devastating results that this expectation can bring. If Habermas's long and complicated theories have taught us this and this alone, they have already made an invaluable contribution to the critical theory of society.

By way of conclusion to this section we can sum up Habermas's overall theory in the following diagram:

Knowledge - constitutive interests	→	The different sciences	Forms of social action
1. Technical: concerned with control and survival.	→	Empirical - Analytical sciences.	→ Labour.
2. Practical: seeking mutual understanding within a common tradition.	→	Historical - Hermeneutical sciences.	→ Social interaction.
3. Emancipatory: freedom from a dogmatic and controlling past.	→	Socially critical sciences.	→ Communication via the ideal speech situation.

3

Praxis and Contemporary Theology

In chapter two we saw something of the background and development of the concept of praxis in philosophy, moving from Aristotle through Marx into the twentieth century. In the course of this overview it became evident that a revolution in the philosophical understanding of praxis occurred with Karl Marx. Some of the implications of this change, initiated by Marx, were developed by the critical theorists of the Frankfurt School in the early part of this century.

It should now be clear that there are two views on the meaning of praxis. The classical view, going back to Aristotle, claims that parxis, though important, is nonetheless subordinated to theory. Pride of place is given to the primacy of theory: theory guides action, action is simply the application of theory. The second view of praxis, which could be called the Critical-Marxist view, affirms the primacy of praxis over theory. In this view praxis is the source, ground and goal of theory, theory is subordinated to critical praxis. It is this second view of praxis that we propose, for reasons that will become clear in the course of this chapter, as more appropriate to the aims of contemporary theology.

This rather rapid survey of the move to praxis calls for some kind of critical evaluation before we look at its implications for theology. An initial reaction to Marx, critical theory and Habermas will help to situate the potential of this movement for theology today. There can be no doubt that these developments do have something to say to theology and its future direction.

Reactions to Marx, Critical Theory and Habermas
Probably the most significant point about Marx's contribution concerns his reflections on praxis. According to R. J. Bernstein, Marx's view on critical praxis 'provides us with some of the most fruitful leads in understanding and criticizing present social reality, for coming to a better grasp of what man is and can become'.[1] This preoccupation with praxis 'must be judged to be one of the richest and most vital orientations of our times'.[2] The radical unity suggested by Marx between theory and praxis, with its attendant attempts to overcome the dichotomy between fact and value, is a turning point in the history of ideas. An equally significant insight in Marx, though perhaps less developed, is his reaction against classical materialism with its mechanistic understanding of reality as something composed of discrete particles. According to classical materialism reality is governed by mechanical laws. Marx is concerned to highlight the fact that reality, especially social reality, is not mechanistically predetermined. Instead it is the praxis of labour that determines the shape of reality and so social reality can be changed. This second insight may be called the principle of change in Marx. Closely related to this is Marx's theory of alienation. Because we shape reality by our praxis, it follows that we are responsible for the alienation that results from praxis . The corollary to this is the claim that people should be able to alter the structures of human alienation. Alienation, therefore, is not something to be blindly accepted; it is rather a challenge to praxis.

These particular insights, which might appear rather commonplace to us today, were quite original in their own times. At the same time, however, it must be acknowledged that they are by no means peculiarly Marxist ideas anymore. They can be found in different shadings in other systems of thought: pragmatism, process philosophy, and the psychoanalytical sciences. Further it should be noted that these insights of Marx are more significant as general orientations than they are, any longer, valuable as specific theses. Indeed, much of the smaller print of Marx's philosophy has come in for serious criticism, something that Marx himself would probably have welcomed. Some of this comes from groups specifically inspired by the general orientation of Marx's principles such as the Frankfurt School of Critical Theory. For example, critical theorists point out that Marx's view of praxis, if pursued too literally, tends somewhat towards *techne* — that is, towards what we commonly call instrumental reason. This is due to the restriction of praxis to labour, understood primarily as the mode of material production. Although Marx does see labour as involving social relationships, these are absorbed in the process of labour as primarily the material production which operates as the basic paradigm for his understanding of praxis.[3] Further, as already noted, critical theorists question the assumption that the development of capitalism, without attention to the socio-cultural dimensions of human existence, would automatically lead to conditions necessary for a classless society. Twentieth-century society is far more complex in its structure, organisation and administration than simply the outcome of the imbalanced material production of labour.

Concerning the principle of change in Marx, namely that social reality is not mechanically determined but changeable, it must be observed that there are apparent inconsistencies in Marx on this point as we noted already in chapter two. In spite of the principle of change Marx persists in claiming: 'It is not the consciousness of men that determines their existence, but their social existence that determines their consciousness.'[4] To hold that the circumstances of life condition consciousness would imply that the individual could not transcend the material conditions of existence. If this were the case humanity would be unable to see beyond the present to demand the possibility of a better future. Is it not precisely this ability of human consciousness to see beyond the present in the experience of praxis that is the basis of change for tomorrow? Marx was right in drawing attention to the influence of social reality upon human consciousness but wrong in insisting that consciousness is restricted by social reality. The only way to resolve this tension is to employ, in the spirit of Marx himself, the principle of a dialectical relation between the apparently opposing tendencies.

Thirdly, at the level of Marx's diagnosis of the sources of alienation, is there not an unrealistic optimism about the capacity of the nature of humanity here? To be sure some forms of alienation can be reduced, indeed eliminated in certain instances. However as Habermas rightly reminds us in this regard: 'Freedom from hunger and toil does not necessarily converge with freedom from slavery and degradation, because an automatic developmental connection between labor and interaction does not exist.'[5] The point here is that the elimination of alienation simply by technology does not necessarily bring freedom at the level of social interaction praxis. The causes of human alienation go far beyond the existing system of property-relations.[6] These causes must include reference to what traditional theology calls 'original sin' and what contemporary theology refers to as 'social sin'.

In addition to these points concerning praxis, change and alienation, reference must be made to the rather obvious fact that the world has changed dramatically since the time of Marx. As a result, Marx's critical theory of political economy belongs to an earlier moment in social development. Here we must remember that Marx's theory was worked out at a time when the Western world was moving into an early phase of industrialisation. Since then science and technology have 'developed' beyond recognition. Instrumental reason rules the day, determines social movements, controls information and distorts symbolic communications in a way that Marx simply could not anticipate. It is these issues that critical theory, especially in the person of Habermas, attempts to overcome.

Over and above these criticisms there is the permanent problem of the anti-religion polemic throughout Marx's writings. This factor does create serious difficulties for any easy alliance between theology and Marx. However, there is no reason why Marx's views on critical praxis, change and alienation cannot be adopted in forms stripped of their crude caricaturing of religion. This process of explicit disassociation from Marx's views on religion would also have to include an equally formal distancing from the Pelagianism which is clearly intrinsic to Marx's views on self-emancipation.

Many of the problems implicit in Marx's understanding of society have been taken up by the Frankfurt School of Critical Theory. Regardless of the ultimate success of critical theory it has to be admitted that the Frankfurt School did at least alert society to some of the incipient contradictions and anomalies that have subsequently become commonplace in contemporary society. Critical theory drew attention to the increasing influence of technology upon the shape of modern society. In this it anticipated the takeover by technical reason of practical reason in the practical ordering and administration of modern society. Further, critical theory alerted society to the myth of 'pure knowledge,' a fiction beloved of many scientists and social theorists in the twentieth century. This particular myth is still with us in many guises: sociology, social science, social biology, technology and modern science. It is this myth that, to a large degree accounts for the reigning divorce between theory and praxis, and the related dichotomy between fact and value. In addition, critical theory has constructively retrieved the value of negative critique as an important instrument for reforming society. The purpose of this insistence by critical theory upon negativity is two-fold. On the one hand it provides a tool for overcoming what Horkheimer calls 'the myth of things as they actually are', a myth which has been bequeathed ironically to us in the twentieth century by enlightenment.[7] On the other hand the social and political mistakes of the past can be avoided with its help. A persistent refusal to identify reason with social reality is present within critical theory so that no easy accommodation can be achieved between the dominant consciousness and society. This particular principle is important today when we consider that the reigning consciousness is largely one of technology. An additional and not insignificant influence inspiring critical theory in this regard was its appropriation of the negative theology of Judaism with its insistence on the non-identity of God and the world, even to the extent of refusing to tolerate the existence of images of God. This particular perception of negativity within Judaism is gaining a new acceptance today from the application of sociology to

Judaism.[8] For critical theory, reason seeks to realise itself within social reality. The task is a project to be realised as much in the future as it is in the present. This refusal to integrate practical reason with society acts as an important corrective against the domination of ideology.

In effect, the major and lasting contribution of critical theory is that it 'marks the beginning of the end of innocent critique'.[9] For too long the impression was given that certain forms of criticism existed without any presuppositions that criticism could be innocent and 'pure', as it were. In fact, what happened was that these forms of criticism were being set up as absolute, and thus the old dogmatism was being replaced by another disguised form of dogmatism. Critical theory unmasks this pretence by subjecting all criticism to its own principle of dialectical negativity while openly acknowledging its own interest in on-going emancipatory praxis.

These positive aspects of classical critical theory must be balanced against some of its more obvious failures. On the one hand critical theory became so preoccupied with its own principles that it lost touch with socio-political praxis on the gound and so failed to achieve any creative unity between its own theory and praxis. Something of this failure can be sensed in Horkheimer's despairing remark: 'If there is anyone to whom we can pass the responsibilities for the message, we bequeath it not to the "masses" not to the individual (who is powerless) but to an imaginary witness − lest it perish with us.'[10] Further, by concentrating on psychological, social and cultural aspects, critical theory ended up neglecting the political-economic dimensions of modern society.[11] In addition this excessive concern with the social, psychological and cultural superstructure ended in too pessimistic a critique of society.[12]

Habermas tries to go beyond the failures of classical theory without however detaching himself altogether from their basic principles. His development of the concern of critical theory not to allow the dominance of *techne* is of particular importance. Habermas's analysis of the supremacy of technical reason in modern society helps us to understand some

of the extraordinary anomalies that beset the latter half of
the twentieth century. Such anomalies include the spending
of more on militarism than on people, the build-up of nuclear
arms that could destroy the earth many times over in the
name of peace, the 'management' of news in the name of
truth, the indiscriminate crossing of geographical boundaries
for the sake of security, and the muffling of truth by government news agencies. These anomalies are, in one way or
another, the result of an all-pervading instrumental rationalis-
ation of society. For Habermas this pervasiveness of the
technocratic consciousness has given rise to 'the repression of
ethics as a category of life'.[13]

This reduction of knowledge to technique is at present
having a devastating effect on the contemporary political
process. Decisions are no longer made through the forum of
public debate. Instead the decision-making process of democracy is taken over by a new breed of technical 'experts' who
decide priorities on the basis of instrumental reason, with
little or no reference to the legitimate demands of practical
reason. A new kind of 'knowledge-industry' prevails that has
become the preserve of the technological consciousness of
the few. It is this primacy of *techne* that has resulted in the
undiscussed commitment of some countries in the western
world to an unrestrained 'defence economy' and/or 'national
security' policies.[14]

In particular, Habermas's theory of knowledge-constitutive-
interest is a valuable epistemological tool for understanding
the cultural crisis of the west. This crisis could be summed up
in the strange paradox that the advances of modern science
of technology have become in many instances more of a
menace to society than a source of genuine progress.[15] The
menace in question is the menace of instrumental reason
divorced from practical and emancipatory interests. In
addition, Habermas's theory of the link between knowledge
and interest is the key to appreciating present-day concern
with emancipation not only in theology but among all human
beings of good will. Liberation movements cannot be dis-
missed simply as passing fads or momentary trends. These
movements, of course, have been heightened by the promise

and potential of modern science and technology. More significant, however, is the fact that this quest for liberation is rooted in humanity's knowledge-constitutive orientation towards human freedom.

Habermas's most significant contribution, however, may well be found in what many regard as also his most serious failure. As already noted, Habermas's complex theory of communicative competence is a warning against any easy resolution of the theory-praxis relationship and against naive programmes of action to solve the problems of the world. The difficulties involved in overcoming the theory-praxis dichotomy and in promoting action for justice should not be underestimated, especially in the political arena.

At the same time, however, it must be admitted that the rationally intricate subtleties of Habermas's theory of communicative competence do seem to have strayed some significant distance from an emancipatory interest.[16] To what extent does his theory of the ideal speech situation lend itself to the practical orientation of what is to be done here and now in a particular situation? What does the ideal speech situation have to say to the concrete circumstances of everyday life?

Charles Davis raises these difficulties with Habermas's attempt to provide a rational grounding for human emancipation. In the first instance Davis doubts that argumentation alone can be the chief means or grounds of a rational consensus on freedom. More important than argumentation is the experience of freedom without which we cannot talk intelligently about emancipation. Secondly, Davis points out that conflicts which may arise in human discourse are usually resolved more effectively at the level of experience and action than argumentation even when ideal circumstances may exist. Thirdly, the elimination of domination does not necessarily lead to agreement in discourse. We are still left with the givenness of great variation in human endowment and the existence of cultural disparity. Much of Habermas's discussion of the ideal speech situation seems to take place in some kind of non-historical situation removed from the ambiguity of the human condition.[17]

The Theory-Praxis Relationship in Theology

This review of the different emphases on praxis in Marx, critical theory and Habermas gives us some sense of the radical changes that have been taking place in social philosophy in the last hundred years or so. At this stage we need to draw up an inventory of the different possibilities that exist concerning the theory-praxis relationship within Christianity, as reflected in theology influenced by these developments. A constructive framework is provided by Matthew Lamb in this regard.[18] Lamb outlines the existence of five models within which we can situate the different possibilities of the theory-praxis relationship for Christian faith. Lamb sees theory as the orientation of the subject towards authentic subjectivity. A summary of Lamb's five models will help to situate the swing in theology towards the primacy of praxis:

1. *The primacy of theory.* This model reflects the Aristotelian emphasis on *theoria*, where theory means knowledge of eternal and immutable truths provided by revelation, presented by the Church and supported by classical metaphysics. In this scheme, praxis is external to theory. Norms for human action come from theoretical knowledge.

2. *The primacy of praxis.* According to this model, theory is only an approximation of what is actually happening in the world. Theory is secondary to practice. Norms for human action are given to us in our emotive-intuitive experiences of life.

3. *The primacy of faith-love.* In this instance Christian faith-love goes beyond theory and praxis. There can be no identity between faith-love and theory-praxis (K. Barth, H. v. Balthasar). Emphasis is placed on the incomprehensible mystery of God and the need for absolute obedience to the word of God. Norms for living can be found only in the paradoxical perspectives of God's self-revelation in the Bible.

4. *Critical theoretic correlation.* Here a critical correlation is understood to exist between Christianity and

human existence. A relationship of continuity within difference between the gospel of Christ and the contemporary situation is developed. This critical relationship is seen to exist on the level of theory (Tracy). The role of theology is to mediate this critical relationship. Norms for action can be found in the mediation of this critical theoretical correlation between Christian faith and life. In effect, praxis is determined by theory.

5. *Critical praxis correlation.* According to this model the critical correlation between Christianity and theory-praxis takes place in praxis: praxis grounds theory. Praxis is the goal and the foundation of theory. In this scheme theory appears as the self-understanding of praxis, the consciousness of what is taking place in Christian praxis. Praxis, therefore, acts as a corrective of theory; praxis brings about change in theory; praxis though inspired by theory is the norm of theory; praxis exercises a critical function *vis à-vis* all theory. Although Lamb does refer to the praxis in question here as one of social transformation alongside religious, moral, intellectual and psychic forms of praxis, more attention might have been given to the emancipatory character of praxis *vis-à-vis* society. Within this fifth model it should be noted that noetic praxis (that is the intellectual praxis of authentic self-transcendence) must be matched by a social, transformative and liberating praxis which, in its turn, generates further theory. To fall short of this would be to miss the radical character of the primacy of praxis in many forms of contemporary theology.[19] It is the praxis of social transformation that generates noetic praxis, including quite often the praxis of personal conversion.

In other words the appeal that is made to the primacy of praxis in liberation and political theology is an appeal primarily to that particular human activity, animated by a radical commitment to the freedom of humanity, that has the power to bring about change in the social situation of suffering humanity in the world, an experience which also affects the agents of this particular praxis. This particular transformative praxis will of course generate its own noetic praxis. The import of praxis here is primarily one of social transformation and not just intellectual activity. The ideal, of course, would be the existence of a creative unity between noetic praxis, social praxis and the emergence of a new noetic praxis. Noetic praxis alone will never change the world. Social praxis that issues in a new noetic praxis will give rise to further change in society which is the object of praxis-grounded political and liberation theologies.

Within the context of this fifth model, which is still only finding its feet and is in need of further refinement, we would propose the following principles as foundational to a social theology of praxis:

a. Praxis does not mean the continuation, implementation or mechanical application of a previously defined theory. Praxis is not about an easy transition from theory to activity. Praxis does not imply mere technique or know-how; nor does it simply mean 'putting faith into practice'; nor is it just about making Christianity relevant and practical.

b. Put positively, praxis is always reflective, dialectical, and intentionally transformative; praxis is always constructively conflictual setting one over against the prevailing social and cultural consciousness; praxis is always liberating and therefore reconciliatory and emancipatory.

c. Praxis arises out of some form of commitment to and solidarity with other human beings, a commitment and solidarity that demands social analysis of the human situation. To this extent praxis originates out of commitment and in theory.

d. Praxis, at least the praxis of liberation and political theology, addresses one or other of the many forms of personal, social or economic evil in the world and is therefore primarily a praxis of liberating transformation.

e. The criterion of authentic praxis whether it be the religious praxis of self-transcendence, the moral praxis of conversion, or the neotic praxis of intellectual growth is the transformative effect it has on the composition of social reality. Praxis therefore always aims at bringing about change in society *and* the individual.

f. The understanding of knowledge and truth operative in the primacy of praxis is one of transformation in contrast to the more traditional understanding of knowledge and truth as simply disclosure or correspondence or conformity or verification. These latter tend to maintain the status quo whereas an understanding of knowledge and truth as transformation challenges theology to go beyond the status quo. Truth is perceived within the experience of bringing about a liberating change in society. Knowledge and truth are now experienced as concommitant to the praxis of personal transformation and social change. Truth is not available over or below or beyond the reflective praxis of individual and social transformation.

g. Lastly, praxis arises out of theory and proceeds to modify that theory by changing the reality from which it arose. As praxis runs its course the originating ground of theory namely social reality is altered, and as modified that social reality becomes the source of a new theory animating a further new praxis. Thus praxis, animated by theory, is always dialectical, effecting change and so generating a new theory.

The value of Lamb's five models is that they illustrate the different shifts that have been taking place in theology in recent times. They alert us to the strengths and weaknesses, the pitfalls and possibilities that exist in determining which direction theology should take in the future. In opting for the primacy of critical praxis as just elaborated upon, we take it to be axiomatic that theology must have some reference to the human, historical, social and cultural situation of humanity in the world. Christian theology is always an incarnate theology: a theology critically correlating the gospel vision with the human situation, creatively inserting the saving message of Jesus into the estranged experience of humanity.

Classical Theology and Praxis-Theology
In the light of this outline of the theory-praxis relationship in theology we must now try to make some assessment of these developments for the self-understanding of theology. The shift initiated by Marx, developed by critical theory and expanded by Habermas cannot be ignored by theology. This shift could be summed up in terms of taking more

seriously some of the basic insights of the Enlightenment while trying to avoid at the same time the obvious flaws of the Enlightenment. This shift in broad terms amounts to the introduction of a new way of understanding the world we live in, a new way of arriving at knowledge, and a new way of coming to know the truth. Obviously these are central concerns not only for philosophy but also for theology. In a sense we are faced with two different ways, perhaps complementary, of understanding the world and arriving at knowledge. These are brought out strikingly by N. Lobkowicz in his important study. *Theory and Practice: History of a Concept from Aristotle to Marx:*

> Aristotle philosophizes out of wonder, out of an intellectual curiosity, which is half awe, half the desire to adjust man's existence to the order of being, the cosmos. Both Hegel and Marx, philosophize out of unhappiness and dissatisfaction, out of the experience that the world is not as it ought to be. . . . In Aristotle nothing is or even can be wrong as it is in its natural state. The problem for Aristotle does not consist in correcting the universe or in making it rational; it consists in discovering its inherent order and rationality. . . . In Hegel almost everything is wrong and consequently has to be *auf gehoben*, transfigured, transformed, revolutionized.[20]

The Aristotelian approach is primarily a contemplative view of knowledge. It operates on the assumption that meaning is given through reflection on the world *as it is*. Knowledge is gained by bringing the intellect into line with the natural, inherent order of the universe. In contrast, Marx refuses to accept the world as he finds it. He senses there is something intrinsically wrong with the world as he experiences it, that the social organisation of human existence could and should be different from the way in fact it is at present. The world, therefore, as we experience it, should be changed and the process of change should be one of 'revolutionary praxis' in contrast to a merely different theoretical reinterpretation of life or just a change of consciousness as was suggested by the Young Hegelians. Here we have what appears to be two distinct approaches to and interpretations of reality, especially social reality. Further, it is precisely these two apparently different approaches that seems to be at issue in the present debate between classical theology and the praxis-oriented political and liberation theologies.

Classical theology seems to be concerned with theoretical interpretation of a given biblical and ecclesial tradition. The task of theology is to support the faith of the Christian community that keeps alive the integrity of this given tradition. By way of reaction to this, it is pointed out that this classical understanding of theology seems to be too theoretical, apparently neglecting the place of praxis in faith itself and leaving the reality of social existence untouched by the gospel and therefore unaltered. Some clarifications are called for here. It must be noted that the origin and continued existence of the Christian tradition was and is the outcome of the praxis of the faith of the community. The praxis of faith is the activity of the human community responding to the gracious action of God mediated by Church and sacrament. The Christian tradition is always a living tradition (*traditio* as distinct from simply *tradita*) supported by the activity of faith. To this extent it is misleading to suggest that classical theology ignores the praxis of faith. Classical theology, perhaps sometimes unknown to itself, lived out of the experience and praxis of the faith of the Christian community. Furthermore, classical theology in its interpretation of tradition did give rise to practice. It inspired, indeed commanded, the performance of charitable deeds and corporal works of mercy. Thus it must be granted that classical theology did have practical consequences. This practical character of the faith of classical theology, as active response to the grace of God mediated by the Christian community and as source of individual acts of charity, must be acknowledged before any fruitful dialogue can take place between classical theology and contemporary praxis-oriented theologies.

What then is the force behind the criticism of praxis

theologies, or more specifically what is the difference between classical theology and praxis-theology? This question can only be answered by taking into account the impact of the Enlightenment and Marx's application of the spirit of the Enlightenment to life as well as the general orientation of subsequent critical theorists. This does not mean that we accept everything that the spirit of the Enlightenment stood for. Indeed we know only too well in retrospect that there was much in the Enlightenment that turned out to be quite destructive of the quality of life and religion. However, the basic insight, that humanity must begin to assume an enlightened responsibility for the shape of the world, remains hauntingly valid to this day. Negatively, it implied that the world is not controlled by nature or blind historical forces or indeed by some capricious interfering God of the gaps. Positively, it implied that humanity can influence the shape and character of the world we live in. This insight was confirmed by developments in subsequent centuries. It has been refined in this century by a growing historical consciousness that we live in a global village which brings with it a new sense of responsibility for self and social determination.

It is this insight and its application by Marx and critical theorists to the character of social existence that is ultimately at issue in the debate between classical theology and praxis theology. The perspectives opened up by the Enlightenment, noted by Marx and developed by critical theorists did not exist for classical theology. In the pre-scientific world of classical theology the quality of social existence was understood as something given by nature, determined by history and fixed by law. As a result the practical activity of faith was not directed to the transformation of the social structure of human existence, which was understood to be fixed in the first instance. Acts of charity inspired by faith were performed principally by individuals and directed towards individuals in need without much attention to structural change through corporate action and its transformative effects. Thus the criticism by praxis-theology that classical theology left the social structure of existence untouched and therefore unaltered is largely true though perhaps historically unfair. It is true in the sense that individual acts of charity did not and could not intend or attempt change in the social structures. It is unfair in the sense that such change was not a possible option in the pre-enlightenment period. Within this shift towards praxis-theology it is possible to discern two movements of enlightenment. The first enlightenment of the eighteenth century was primarily an attempt to free reason from the controlling influences of nature, history and authority. It did this mistakenly, by reducing all theory to empirical method, thereby excluding all reference to the religious dimension of experience. The spirit of this first Enlightenment is summed up in Kant's famous declaration: *aude, sape;* have courage to use your own understanding. This first Enlightenment was, therefore, an Enlightenment of theory. The second Enlightenment, symbolised in the views of Marxist-critical theorists, heightened by the potential for emancipation released by modern science and technology and sharply focused by the present awful prospect of nuclear destruction, is primarily about freeing human action from the maintaining forces of nature, history and authority. The spirit of this second Enlightenment might be summed up in the imperative: *aude, emancipe*; have courage to determine through emancipatory action your destiny in a manner that respects the destiny of others. This second Enlightenment, therefore, is an Enlightenment of praxis. The task of praxis-theology is to respond to the enormous collective challenges posed by the second Enlightenment in a way that avoids the errors of the first Enlightenment.

Praxis-theology is concerned therefore to acknowledge the advances as well as the mistakes that have taken place in the world since the first Enlightenment. It is a call for the adoption of a new responsibility through social praxis by the Christian community for the shape of the world we live in. It is a demand to energise the vision of the gospel by activating a new social praxis proportionate to that gospel vision. In other words, where classical theology was content to promote an individual and noetic praxis of the faith, praxis-theology wants to engage in a corresponding corporate and socially transformative praxis of the faith. While classical theology was satisfied to live with the social situation as something given and therefore determined, praxis-theology wishes to initiate a process of social change as something intrinsic to the demands of the gospel itself. Insofar as classical theology worked out of a tradition that appeared to be primarily interpretative, praxis-theology aims to become an action-based enterprise as both the goal and basis of that tradition.

Implications of the Shift to Praxis for Theology today
An outline of some of the implications of this shift may help to sum up the relationship that we now see existing between praxis, critical theory and theology. These implications can be conveniently drawn together under the headings of epistemology, anthropology, the sociology of knowledge, and the ongoing dialogue between critical theory and theology. At the epistemological level we must begin to move away from a purely contemplative view of knowledge. This latter view implies that knowledge is derived merely from an observation 'of things as they actually are' (Horkheimer) or even worse that knowledge is a carbon copy of external reality as it is given. G. E. M. Anscombe points out:

> Certainly in modern philosophy we have an incorrigibly contemplative conception of knowledge. Knowledge must be something that is judged as such by being in accordance with the facts. The facts, reality, are prior, and dictate what is to be said if it is knowledge and this is the explanation of the utter darkness in which we found ourselves.[21]

This passive, spectator, empiricist, objectivist view of knowledge completely ignores the part played by the subject, especially the intentionality of the subject, in the genesis of all human knowledge. Even more seriously this contemplative conception of knowledge neglects the human, historical and social conditions of the subject in the search for knowledge. The subject that knows is always a subject immersed in some form of human estrangement, historical oppression and social injustice. Thus the dynamic intentionality of the subject will always include, as Habermas has so helpfully reminded us, a critical moment of interest in the emancipation of social reality. All human knowledge has an underlying thrust towards emancipation. This implies that knowledge is advanced in the experience of social praxis. Knowledge emerges out of a creative unity that exists between social praxis and noetic praxis. The separation of knowledge from social praxis runs the risk of supporting the social status quo and legitimating some other interests that are less than emancipatory.

Linked to this praxis-centred understanding of knowledge is the presence of an equally different view of what constitutes the truth. In many traditional epistemologies, such as empiricism or even critical realism, the model of truth which is operative is one of disclosure. In a praxis-centred understanding of knowledge the model of truth is one of transformation. Truth is perceived in the experience of social transformation. Truth is tied up with social transformation. Truth, within this particular perspective, appears as much a reality to be discovered through the creation of a new future as it is a reality given in the past. This newly emerging epistemology has much to offer theology and its particular understanding of the meaning of religious knowledge.

In the first instance the idea of knowledge as located in the experience of social praxis safeguards theological doctrine from appearing as some kind of élitist *gnosis* and the obvious temptation this brings towards gnosticism. Theological doctrine is never merely information but also and more fundamentally a challenge to promote and activate in social praxis the good news of salvation which it embodies. Secondly the emancipatory character of all knowledge reminds theology of its basic soteriological theme. Theology that loses contact with the gift and task of salvation is no longer a truly Christian theology always concerned with the grace of God, '*propter nos et propter nostram salutem*'. Further, we should not forget how Paul reminds us that the saving truth of the Gospel is a truth that will set us free. Thirdly, there is no reason why the transformative model of truth should not be seen as a necessary complement and corrective to the more traditional model of truth as disclosure. The truth revealed in Jesus is at one and the same time a moment of disclosure and of transformation. For the Christian, the disclosure of truth involves transformation and the truth that emerges in transformation comes as disclosure. A creative tension exists within Christianity between the present and future that parallels this complementary relationship between disclosure and transformation. While it is important to acknowledge that Christology is the basis of our eschatological vision, it is equally important to moderate our christological claims by that vision. The disclosure model of truth tends to leave things as they are, affirming the present in a way that neglects the future. The transformative model promotes change within our world. What is needed in Christian theology today is a creative unity of disclosure and transformation, directed towards a concern for change within continuity. Fourthly, the shift from knowledge as contemplation to knowledge as praxis puts the emphasis in theology where it most properly belongs, namely in the transforming experience of actually living out the gospel at the intersecting levels of individual, social and noetic praxis. In other words, the peculiar perspectives of theology contained in revelation (*Deus revelatus et absconditus*), christology (death and resurrection), soteriology (salvation affecting the present and future), and eschatology (tension between 'the already' and 'the not yet') seem more compatible with the epistemological orientations of knowledge and truth as entailing both transformative praxis and disclosive experience rather than knowledge and truth as simply contemplative.

On the anthropological level praxis theology implies a change of focus in our understanding of human identity which is closely bound up with the epistemological shift just outlined. The classical emphasis on the individual as knower must make room for an equal emphasis on the 'individual as agent'. Here more attention should be given to the Hegel-Marx insight that the individual *is* what he or she does, that the person becomes what she or he performs. Action as much as knowledge shapes human identity: in a limited but important sense the human subject is what it does, activity specifies human identity, I am what I do. Of course, it must be acknowledged that the individual is more than simply what he or she does. While it is necessary to point out that the individual cannot be reduced without remainder to action, it must also be emphasised, as a corrective to essentialism, that action is an integral element in the coming to be of human identity. Further, and this has to be said if we are to avoid the individualistic excesses of some forms of existentialism, not only the identity but also the dignity of the individual and his or her belongingness to a larger household of reality is revealed by what he or she does in this life.

As before care must be taken not to set up some kind of false opposition or dichotomy between the 'individual as agent' and the 'individual as knower'. Instead we wish to suggest that these two dimensions of human identity are mutually complementary and supportive. As we have seen so frequently throughout this chapter, the praxis of the individual is always animated by some form of knowledge. Knowledge activates praxis and praxis generates new knowledge. This particular relationship between praxis and knowledge is all the more important if we are to promote a responsible social praxis as distinct from an irresponsible mindless activism or mere *techne* divorced from practical reason.

Further, we must remember in this anthropological context that the 'individual as agent' is always a social agent. The subject as agent grows and develops out of social congress with other subjects. Human agency, subjectivity and selfhood are a social reality in process. To this extent the individual as agent is always situated historically in a particular social situation. The agent as subject is part of a wider network of complex social relations. Part of Marx's essential contribution to our understanding of reality is the suggestion that the praxis of individuals shapes the social character of those institutions that make up the fabric of life. For Marx, social reality is in some sense an objectification of the social praxis of individual agents. These 'objectifications' are not necessarily determined; they can in fact be changed or at least altered by the social praxis of human agents. By implic-

ation every individual as agent is faced sooner or later with
the decision whether he or she wishes to promote or change
the objectified structures of social praxis. This decision is by
no means a neutral one especially when we take into account
the fact that these objectified structures are in many instances
the source of social estrangement, discrimination and oppression.

The development of this anthropology appears, like the
above epistemology, to be quite in keeping with the overall
direction of Christian faith. For example, any adequate
description of the identity of individual Christian faith must
surely appeal to the individual as agent as much as it does
to the individual as knower. To describe the Christian faith
only as knowledge would be to lose sight of the essentially
performative character of Christian faith which of course is
informed by knowledge. Further, the challenge to the individual as agent to change the social structures of life through
praxis is a powerful reminder to the Christian of his or her
responsibility to confront the reality of social sin in our
world. Christian faith cannot remain unaffected by the latter,
especially since it is now more possible than ever before to
modify some of these sinful social structures. The individual
as responsible agent of faith can no longer remain indifferent
to those objectified sinful social structures that enslave,
dehumanise or oppress, whether consciously or otherwise,
our brothers and sisters in Christ. Faith challenges the
Christian community in a spirit of solidarity with the suffering body of Christ in the world to the performance of a new
social praxis. In addition it must be pointed out that the
major criticisms of Christianity down through the centuries,
and especially in the twentieth century, have been aimed at
particular forms of praxis, or the lack of them, in the face
of pressing socio-ethical-political problems, rather than at
the particular cognitional claims of faith. The crisis of faith
in the past and present was and is provoked more often
by a particular praxis than simply by a particular theoretical
stance.

Praxis-theology works out of and depends upon social
analysis. Praxis-theology clearly is not to be identified with

social analysis. The role of social analysis is diagnostic, exposing the sources and causes of human alienation in society that contradict the vision of the gospel. This relationship between praxis-theology and social analysis is becoming more obvious and more universally accepted today. An important subdivision of social analysis is the sociology of knowledge.

The sociology of knowledge is a relatively new science. Its basic insight is the recognition that human consciousness is shaped, at least to some degree, by social reality. This insight is a modified echo of Marx. The sociology of knowledge was developed as a science by Max Scheler, W. Dilthey and K. Mannheim. A more recent statement of the basic thesis of the sociology of knowledge is the claim that: 'No human thought ... is immune to the ideologizing influences of its social context.'[22]

The sociology of knowledge is concerned to bring out the close relationship that exists between knowledge and the social context in which it arises. Knowledge is not neutral or value-free. Instead all knowledge tends to embody the social circumstances and conditions of its time. To this extent knowledge tends to be bound up with the vested interests of the social reality it embodies and, therefore, tends to promote the status quo. According to the sociology of knowledge, ideas as such do not change the circumstances of life; theory as such is not necessarily the best way of dealing with the crises of life. Why? Because the ideology supporting social reality tends to rub off, unconsciously or otherwise, on our knowledge and understanding of human existence.

The sociology of knowledge therefore is of vital interest to praxis-theology not only because it confirms the basic orientation of praxis-theology but also because it alerts praxis-theology to the possibility that its own theological theory-praxis may include an ideological component from social reality, including the social reality of institutionalised Christianity. Thus praxis-theology will want to apply the sociology of knowledge to its own theological operations in theory-praxis. This means that praxis-theology will want to examine its own theory-praxis lest it be infected by the ideology, past or present, of social reality both outside and inside Christianity. If praxis-theology is to succeed and to be credible it must be prepared to apply internally what it seeks to do externally.

Many will react against theology that seeks to change social reality, especially the social reality of institutionalised Christianity. They will argue that the social structures of human existence, especially those of the Church, must be safeguarded, protected and maintained in existence. In response to this understandable though unacceptable reaction the following points should be kept in mind.

Social reality as we know it and experience it, perhaps even more visibly so today, is out of joint, dislocated and painfully fragmented. It does not require too much ingenuity to realise that there is something amiss in our world today whether one lives in the first world or the third world. In the first world we are becoming more and more aware of realities like the systematic distortion of communications and the truth, the predominance of menacing technology, the ever-increasing psychological exhaustion of a consumerism-greed gone mad, the creeping dissatisfaction with the plastic culture of modernity, and the growing spiritual poverty (hunger) aggravated by the myth of endless material progress. Though these particular ills pall in comparison to the ravages of third world hunger, poverty and oppression with their causal connection with material extravaganza of the first world, both realities in their own way witness to the malaise of modernity. This kind of common diagnosis by social analysis and the sociology of knowledge is the subject matter of a praxis-oriented theology. To wish to safeguard, protect and maintain in existence this kind of social reality, existence *as it is*, is to end up endorsing, however unwittingly, a social situation that is glaringly sinful. It is to acquiesce, more often than not unconsciously, in sin.

To plead that this social reality is the outcome of original sin and therefore must be accepted is to provide a good example of the kind of thing that the sociology of knowledge warns us against. This use of the dogma of original sin is an illustration of how theological theory can assume the ideological colouring of social reality. One of the purposes of the doctrine of original sin was to counteract Pelagian tendencies and to highlight humanity's need of redemption in Christ. Indeed the doctrine of original sin only makes sense in the context of the salvation brought by Christ. Isolated from the grace of salvation in Christ this doctrine can become ideological. Salvation without reference to Christ is impossible but salvation in and through cooperation with the grace of Christ is possible. The whole point of the doctrine of salvation is to bring about a change from the old order of sin into the new order of grace. The reality of sin in the world, both individual and social, can be modified by the grace of Christ in the world which animates not only individual but also social praxis. To claim otherwise is to come close to the theological howler made recently by the neo-conservative author Michael Novak who in his efforts to justify capitalism let slip:

> The greatest single temptation for Christians is to imagine that the salvation won by Jesus has altered the human situation. Many attempt to judge the world by the standards of the gospel, as though the world were ready to live according to them. . . The Incarnation obliges us to reduce our noblest expectations, so to love the world as to fit a political economy to it, nourishing all that is best in it. . .[23]

Surely Novak doesn't *really* believe that the motive of the Incarnation was 'to reduce our noblest expectations.' Further, has Novak forgotten altogether the teaching of the Council of Trent on the nature of justification?

Of course it must be acknowledged that not all social reality is sinful. To the contrary the gains of the past must be preserved while the ills of the present must be changed by social praxis. The question of what must be preserved within tradition, sacred and secular, is of course as important as the question about what must be changed through social praxis. And yet care must be taken not to allow the hermeneutical question to become an excuse — or worse, an ideology — for the postponement of social praxis. The hard-won gains of yesterday are the theory of today's social praxis in preparation for the creation of a worthy tomorrow. Social analysis and the sociology of knowledge are important tools to help praxis-theology effect this creation of a better future in fidelity to the vision and praxis of the Kingdom of God revealed by Jesus.

Finally, if theology, especially praxis-theology, is to influence the shape of society to come (that is, to assure some kind of social significance as distinct from appearing as a merely private affair), then it must take discerning account of the broad principles of critical theory. This will require a process of distancing itself at the same time from the more obvious defects that we have already alluded to. Some kind of correlation between critical theory and praxis-theology seems not only possible but desirable.

The prominence of ideology critique within critical theory, which is so important in trying to diagnose the contemporary crisis within the western world, provides an important context for praxis-theology within which to recover the prophetic, apocalyptic and eschatological resources of the biblical vision. We should remember that the dialectical negativity of critical theory was inspired, in part at least, by the prophetic tradition of Judaism. At the same time this particular aspect of critical theory is also a timely reminder for praxis-theology to guard against any attempt at identifying theological reason (salvation) with social reality (liberation). Further, critical theory, with its critique of pure theory, its reaction against positivism and its unmasking of instrumental reason will protect theology from degenerating into an ideological superstructure within society and the Church.

However, the major contribution that critical theory can make to praxis-theology lies in the area of soteriology. This is especially true of the early Frankfurt School of Critical Theorists. While J. B. Metz rightly warns against any easy reduction of redemption to emancipatory theory-praxis,[24] E. Schillebeeckx points out with equal justification the impossibility of believing in a Christianity which is not, at least, at one with the universal movement to emancipate humanity.[25]

An important point of convergence as well as difference exists between critical theory and the praxis-theology of salvation. A convergence can be found in the emancipatory interest that guides critical theory and the liberating power that proceeds from the gospel of salvation in Christ Jesus. At the same time major points of difference exist between critical theory and praxis-theology which cannot be glossed over. Critical theory is intent upon self-liberation, replacing the *Deus Salvator* (God, the Saviour) by the *Homo Emancipator* (man, the liberator). Praxis-theology, however, insists that liberating salvation comes from God and is effected ultimately only by God. This particular insistence must not be taken as denigration of the role that the individual and society must play through social praxis in accepting God's grace of salvation. To the contrary, humanity is called 'in Christ' to partner the history of liberating salvation, to be the cooperators with God in effecting the New Creation. For the Christian, to exist is to co-exist with Christ in the task of working for the Kingdom of God. This call to partnership, to be co-creators and co-redeemers 'in Christ' does not diminish but rather increases humanity's social responsibility. Secondly, critical theory muffles 'the silent sufferings of the inconsolable pain of the past,'[26] forgetting the price paid by past victims for present successes. A praxis-soteriology operates out of 'a backward solidarity' with the silent dead as well as 'a forward solidarity' with future generations unified by the liberating and saving memory of the Crucified Jesus.[27]

In spite of these serious misgivings it must be admitted that there is also a sense in which praxis theology needs critical theory. Praxis theology must be protected by critical theory against proposing naive solutions in theory-praxis to the social problems that beset the world today. Theology does not have any privileged access to political solutions over and above the ordinary means available through social analysis and critical rationality. What theology does have is a vision of hope, centred in the person of Christ that generates a liberating praxis in pursuit of the Kingdom of God as present gift and future promise. In pursuing this vision, theology must remind the Christian community that it lives 'in-between-the-times' of the first and second coming of Christ. Critical theory can help theology in this task because: 'Critical theory is not a rounded theory as much as it is a tactic — a sort of interim ethic, a way of waiting without idols in a time of eschatological postponement'.[28]

At the same time, there is an important sense in which it can be said that critical theory with its excessive emphasis on negativity needs the counter-balancing influence of Christian theology with its redemptive message of final meaning. This strong emphasis on negativity is responsible for the pessimism that can be found among the early critical theorists. Something of this need for a theological perspective of final meaning seems to have been sensed by Adorno when he wrote: 'The only philosophy which can be responsibly practised in the face of despair is the attempt to view all things as they would present themselves from the standpoint of redemption.'[29]

An additional factor in working out this correlation between critical theory and praxis-theology concerns the social significance of theological statements about salvation. Critical theory challenges theology to account in praxis for its claims that all are called to freedom 'in Christ', that salvation has already taken place 'in Christ', that humanity and history have been saved 'in Christ', that the world is destined 'in Christ', and that all who belong to Christ are a New Creation. Such soteriological themes of the gospel come under scrutiny today not only by critical theory but by all who look at Christianity from the outside. Do these doctrinal claims have any critical import for society? Does the gospel really have an emancipatory thrust in praxis that affects the social situation of humanity? Is the orthodoxy of 'salvation in Christ' simply a matter of faith without an *ortho-praxis*? Is redemption just a theory about the next life without any basis in present experience and social praxis? Is salvation simply a spiritual and private affair between the individual and God without reference to the rest of humanity? Through such questions critical theory and praxis theology can communicate even though ultimately their perspectives are fundamentally different.

Social Analysis and Process Thought serving Praxis

One of the great contributions of critical theory to our understanding of historical and social existence is its dogged refusal to accept the status quo. Critical theorists have consistently reacted against the temptation to accept an easy alliance between reason and social reality. In this they also refuse to accede to naive confirmation and correspondence theories of truth. In particular they have highlighted the serious consequences that follow from allowing *techne* to take over from *praxis*. These include a glaring dichotomy between fact and value, is and ought, the descriptive and prescriptive in approaching life itself.

It is against the background of this negative but constructive stance that critical theorists have insisted on the importance of praxis. Within this perspective praxis becomes the guide, norm and goal of good theory. This recognition of the primacy of praxis, however, is only a beginning and as such calls for a deeper understanding of the object of praxis. If praxis is to succeed then there must be some overall grasp of the social realities that have to be changed. The primacy of praxis in theory demands some form of social analysis in the first place. Praxis must be based on and informed by social analysis. Social analysis must become an essential element in the theory inspiring *praxis*. The praxis of transformation will succeed only to the extent that it properly understands the intricacies of the situation that needs to be changed. Coming to grips with the complexity of the social situation is itself something that is coloured by the particular assumptions we bring to bear within our analysis. The way we understand reality shapes the way we set about changing the world through praxis. Indeed, the overall framework within which social analysis is carried out will have a distinct bearing on the kind of praxis that is prompted by one's analysis. Not only is social analysis important for praxis but the particular understanding we have of social reality is equally significant for praxis.

This chapter sets out to provide in outline a social analysis of the contemporary world in which we live. It will address some of the problems that have accompanied the rise of modern science and technology in this century as well as focusing attention on certain aspects of social, political and cultural life in our time. In addition, this chapter will focus on some of the presuppositions underlying our understanding of these areas of life. It will indicate how such assumptions must be modified if social praxis is to succeed. The purpose of this chapter is to lay the foundations for an effective praxis by offering a social analysis of the contemporary world and proposing a particular way of understanding reality that is more in touch with human experience and more conducive to the demands of social praxis.

A Social Analysis of the Contemporary Situation

There can hardly be any doubt that the contemporary situation of humanity in the Western world is in a serious state of crisis: scientific, social, ecological, nuclear, economic, political and cultural. Equally the need for some form of critical social analysis with a view to changing this situation is fairly self-evident today. Further, theology cannot pretend to be indifferent to this serious state of affairs. Indeed, theology knows only too well that it is part of the crisis in so far as it expresses itself through social, political and cultural forms that are now being radically called into question. Theology also knows that it is part of the global crisis in the western world to the extent that it continues to support both systems and institutions which maintain the crisis in existence. It was for this reason that Pope Paul VI could write in his own prophetic way back in 1971:

It is up to Christian communities to analyse with objectivity the situation that is proper to their own country, to shed on it the light of the gospel's unalterable words, to draw principles of reflection, norms of judgment and directives of action from the social teaching of the Church.[1]

Our social analysis here can only be undertaken in broad strokes and then only in reference to the first world of the post-industrial west. We will begin with a sample of the issues emerging in science and technology, and then move on to look at some of the social, political and cultural aspects of contemporary consciousness. Attention will be focused primarily on the problems emanating from the so-called developments that have been taking place in these areas of life.

The meteoric developments of science and technology in this century are quite staggering: electronics, nuclear science, microphysics, computers and biophysics. It is only now, in the last quarter of this century, that people are beginning to realise the full implications of these so-called advances. The rapid rise of science to fame has suddenly become a matter of serious concern, a concern centred less on the success of science itself and more on the implications of these successes on the larger issues of life itself.

In the nineteenth century and the first half of this century science moved rather quickly to the centre of the stage and began to assume a new importance and responsibility for the well-being of the world. Promises were made in terms of controlling the blind forces of nature, eliminating illness and disease, and creating a new freedom for determining the destiny of the human race. A battery of new myths was suddenly generated by science: the promise of endless progress, the possibility of unlimited growth, and the prospect of creating a new world. In addition science began to set itself up as the arbiter of what constitutes the real and the true by absolutising the scientific method. Access to reality was available only through the scientific method. In the interests of objectivity, science claimed to be a value-free, detached and neutral observer in coming to know the way things really are.

With the passage of time, however, some of these claims began to fade and be questioned on different fronts. Was it really possible to control nature without having due regard for the character of the environment itself? Could science really heal humanity without attending to the subjectivities of those in need of healing? Is the destiny of the human race just another object that can be manipulated by the controls of science? Gradually, it became clear that progress was something that had to be monitored by reference to factors beyond the empirical competence of science: the unity of the human race, the needs of human subjectivity, and the nature of culture itself. Further, it began to emerge that there are in fact certain constraints on the possibility of growth imposed by nature herself: the ozone level and ecological harmony. Natural resources are limited and if this fact is not respected by science the equilibrium of the environment will be in danger of being irreversibly damaged. Already we know that the domination of nature is giving rise to the destruction of certain fundamental elements of life itself. In addition the possibility of creating a new world by science alone can no longer be taken seriously.

Perhaps the most serious mistake made by science in this century was (still is?) the presumption that it could function as if it were independent, neutral and value-free. In fact, the scientist is not the cold detached clinical observer, that some would have us believe, who operates in a vacuum without reference to a world of values. To the contrary the scientist, as Whitehead and Polanyi frequently remind us, presupposes the existence of the meaning, truth and value in the pursuit of his work; explicit scientific knowledge usually takes place within a larger horizon that is tacitly known by the scientist. The fatal flaw in the development of modern science has been the attempt to isolate itself from what Habermas calls, as we have seen in chapter two, 'the knowledge-constitutive-interests' of humanity, society and nature. It is this development of independence by science that has led to the separation of *techne* from praxis and given rise to the alleged social and political innocence of science. The removal of science from the larger realities of life such as the needs of individuals as subjects, the development of society and respect for the eco-system, is responsible for many of the present-day ambiguities of science. These ambiguities derive in large measure, as the critical theorists forewarned us, from the idolisation of instrumental reason and the demise of practical reason. Most of all it is this isolationism that has allowed science with its promise of security for humanity to become a menacing threat in different ways to the very existence of our globe today: ecological and nuclear. More and more it is becoming clear that much of the technological progress we rate so highly today has brought with it a loss of human values, and the liberation it was expected to bring has become oppressive and enslaving.[2]

The time has come to recognise once and for all that science deals with only a part — not the whole — of reality. Science must be guided by considerations that embrace the whole rather than simply specialised segments of reality. Further, the individual scientist as such cannot exempt himself or herself from responsibility for the social and political implications of his or her work. There is no neutral, value-free zone from which the scientist can conduct his or her research. Further, it must be continually emphasised that science is not an end in itself but rather an integral part of that corporate task facing humanity in the challenge to charter a future that is humanly just, socially equitable, and environmentally sustainable. Within this larger task it is quite clear that the scientific enterprise contains within itself an enormous potential for good or evil in our world. Modern science is fraught with a terrifying ambiguity, an ambiguity that can only be removed by way of reference to that which lies beyond the empirical enclave of science itself: human subjectivity, the needs of society, and the interests of the global village. Left to its own lonely resources science is in danger of reaping havoc in our world today; situated within the larger whole of collective responsibility for the future of one world it is capable of contributing handsomely to the creation of a more human society.

It would be wrong to suggest that science developed this

dangerous spirit of autonomy on its own, in spite of what scientists would like us to believe. Instead it is much nearer the truth to suggest that science in spite of itself was influenced in its development by the surrounding social, political and cultural attitudes of this century. A brief outline of some of these attitudes will show that problems of modern science are merely symptomatic of a wider malaise.

One of the outstanding characteristics of contemporary society is the strong emphasis placed on individualism: the human rights and freedoms of all living persons. These hard-won gains, centred around the uniqueness of the individual, rank among the great achievements of the western world. As such, they must be safeguarded from attacks by ruthless institutions, right-wing governments, and state-run socialism. At the same time it must be acknowledged that there are limits to individualism. The rights of individuals exist always in relation to the rights of others and the freedoms of individuals are restricted and enriched by the freedoms of others. What has tended to happen, however, in contemporary society is that we have had the development of a type of individualism which takes no account of the wider community at large. As a result the good of others is disregarded in favour of the sole good of the individual. This shows itself in different philosophies operating within society, summed up in the crude slogans of today: 'everyone for himself in the secular city'; 'the name of the game is the survival of the fittest'; 'doing your own thing' or doing 'whatever floats your boat'. These slogans can be seen to operated in the ruthless and competitive philosophy of 'looking after number one' at all costs and in the extraordinary emphasis given in society to the 'ethic of achievement' and the adulation of 'personal success'.

> The doctrine of achievement has produced our modern efficient-oriented society in which people are constrained to make progress and be successful ... to justify themselves. In the process their real selves and, what is worse, the real selves of their children, disappear under the heap of achievements or their heap of failures.[3]

This kind of individualism which is so rampant in the twentieth century is a far cry from the rights and freedoms of individuals that were envisaged in the eighteenth century. Individualism that rides roughshod over the rights and freedoms of others within community can no longer be accepted or tolerated by society. The individual is only an individual in relation to others. Indeed the individual is constituted in his or her subjectivity in dependence on and in relation with other subjects. As such, the individual is thoroughly social and cannot exist or survive outside the community of other individuals.

An offshoot of the individualism in modern society is the promotion of a highly competitive spirit as something virtuous. This competitive spirit in turn produces a ruthless and aggressive approach to life that has little respect for the sensitivities of others. The 'hard-sell' knows no limits and is admired, indeed promoted, in certain forms of business today. Success is achieved more often than not at the expense and exploitation of others. As long as our world remains unequally divided into a first world of overproduction and a third world of underdevelopment with the excesses of increasing richness and poverty, growing unemployment, illiteracy and violence, 'successes' and 'achievements' remain at most an ambiguous experience. It is no longer possible to live our lives in blissful neglect or deliberate forgetfulness of the gross inequalities that exist in our world today. The fact is that such inequalities can and should be significantly reduced. This does not mean that we are suggesting in some idle romantic view of things that all differences between human beings can be overcome. There are, however, certain basic needs like food and shelter, health and education, employment and housing, that are the rights of every human being on this planet. The human race is indivisibly one and all human beings are inter-related and as such belong to one and the same organic whole and family. It is this unity of the human family that is offended by certain forms of a ruthless, competitive spirit which is at present so dominant in the commercial sector of contemporary society.

These aspects of science and society are paralleled by the

existence of other similar but equally questionable attitudes present in the world of politics. For example, in the area of economics governments persist in announcing policies that claim to increase the GNP, advance the standard of living and promise 'more for less'. These particular policies are founded on a number of questionable premises: that there are inexhaustible natural resources available and that such progress is necessarily a good thing. In the first place, all the facts now suggest that the natural resources of the earth are quite limited. Related to this is the generally accepted view that the exploitation of natural resources has already exceeded safe limits. Secondly, there is the assumption that governments and politicians can exploit these natural resources without regard to the balance of nature or what Whitehead liked to call the 'feelings' (prehensions) of nature itself. The world of nature can no longer be treated simply as an object available for external manipulation. More and more it is becoming clear that humanity must learn to relate to nature and live in harmony with nature. Without attention to the sensibilities of nature, the future of the human species is in danger of extinction. The ecological question is no longer simply the curious preserve of the naturalist. Instead, the unity that exists between natural life and human life is something that must not only be respected but restored in the future if we are to ensure the survival of the human race. Governments will have to abandon their exploiting approach towards nature, and the accompanying politics of unreasonable promises that follows from this aggressive stance will have to be challenged more realistically in the future.

Another disturbing aspect of contemporary politics in the western world is the massive amount of centralisation and bureaucratisation that has taken place. This regrettable development has had the effect of pushing the individual more and more away from the centre to the margin of the political process, and this in turn has given rise, for many, to a sense of alienation from the decision-making process and to a feeling of very little personal responsibility for the overall good of society. The end result of this is the fragmentation of politics into élitist power groups and pressure groups. The common good becomes the good of a privileged minority which really means that the good of the whole is reduced to the good of a few. This is most evident when decisions are taken by governments on the advice of so-called technical experts, a new generation of 'how to' experts who operate with little or no regard for the good of the whole. Such decisions are more often than not based on the primacy of *techne* over praxis, of instrumental reason over practical reasons, and of means over ends.

The clearest example of this is to be found in the decisions taken by governments in regard to military defence, especially in terms of nuclear arms. These decisions are made for governments by a powerful minority without recourse to the wishes of the majority of the democratically elected representatives of the people and without public discussion of the issues involved. For example, the British parliament did not formally discuss the build-up of nuclear arms that had been going on for fifteen years prior to 1980. When such political decisions are subsequently challenged by the majority they are usually justified by an appeal to the ideology of protecting national security, an ideology which can and has been made to justify anything and everything. When the issue becomes a matter of public concern governments have recourse to the systematic distortion of the truth and the employment of language games. The public are informed for example that the nuclear arms race is necessary 'for the sake of peace' in the world and that deterrency has 'maintained peace' since the second world war. What kind of peace are we talking about that is brought about by the horror of nuclear arms? Can we talk about a peace that is forced upon us through a process of terrorising humanity with the prospect of a nuclear holocaust? Is there really peace in our world when as a result of the nuclear arms race the poor become poorer and their needs are passed over as secondary? This kind of political rhetoric reached an all-time low when President Reagan announced the deployment of one hundred MX missiles in the name of peace and then went on to associate such an act with religion:

Let us work for peace and as we do, let us remember the
lines of the famous hymn:
'O God of love, O king of peace,
Make wars throughout the world to cease.'[4]

The end result of these developments in politics is the
alienation of the individual from the political process,
an increasing lack of participation in decision-making
institutions, a growing sense of apathy and cynicism *vis-à-vis*
anything and everything political, and lastly a serious crisis
of confidence in political leadership and authority.

These developments in politics are by no means unrelated
to some of the attitudes we have already seen associated with
modern science and society. Many of the 'achievements' of
modern governments such as the creation of a thriving
economy, the establishment of a high GNP and the development of a strong defence system are now seen to be viable
only at the expense and exploitation of others: the third
world, the poor and the weak. Indeed, many of the structures that citizens took great pride in promoting through
the political process are now seen to be something of an
embarrassment because of their adverse effect on the rest
of the world. The underlying problem in modern politics
is the subtle removal of the individual from personal participation in responsibility for public policy. This removal
of the individual, which amounts to a separation of the
individual from the political community, thwarts the objectives of the democratic process: social identity, belongingness,
participation, and responsibility.

Moving into the area of culture we can detect other
developments that are related to many of these issues in
science, society and politics. The contemporary situation
in which we live has been characterised as a one-dimensional
culture. The only dimension that seems to matter any more
is that of the infectious cycle of production and consumption
or, as Gabriel Marcel and others like to put it, the primacy
of 'having' over 'being'. We live in a world today that is
fuelled by a frenzied consumerism. This consumption is kept
on the boil by technical developments. In fact, technical

advance and the consumerist thirst seem to be related parts of one and the same vicious circle. Concern with technique and the passion of consumerism feed upon each other and thereby sustain each other in existence.

At the technical level, contemporary culture has become obsessed with 'technique', 'know-how', 'skill', 'instruments', and 'expertise'. The precise purpose of these technical skills is something that is often quite unclear. Much more important is the technical production of means with little regard to their ends. Indeed, one of the more disturbing features of this dominant technical-culture is the amount of research that is funded on a value-free basis as if there was some clinical, neutral vantage point from which to view things. What is perhaps most alarming is the way the passion for technical production — electronic, computer and socio-biological — has significantly outstripped the human, spiritual, and psychological needs of humanity. This technical culture has become the dominant horizon of contemporary experience, determining the way we live and controlling our leisure hours. As Langdon Gilkey points out:

> Technical culture is voracious, devouring; it consumes all other technical aspects of culture in its maw by turning everything else into a skill, a knowledge of how to do it, a means.[5]

The other side of contemporary culture is its consumerist passion. Technical production generates a momentum towards consumption. Production is for consumption and consumption demands 'more' production. A continuous process of rudderless 'turn-over' is set in motion, symbolised in the endless consumption of 'throw-away' and 'disposable' commodities. Contemporary culture is a consumerist culture that has created a new need in the life of humanity: possessing, having, and hoarding. Marcuse observes:

> The need for possessing, consuming, handling, and constantly renewing the gadgets, devices, instruments, engines, offered to and imposed upon the people for using these wares at the danger of one's own destruction has become a 'biological' need.[6]

This new dependency of humanity on the turnover of the market-place does not meet the real needs of humanity. The consumerist experiences of 'having' all ends up as a demeaning experience of 'having' nothing. A vacuum is created at that point in human experience that is most in need of spiritual substance and fullness. The consumerist satisfaction of what Marcuse calls humanity's 'biological need' frustrates humanity's deeper 'spiritual needs'. Consumerism blunts our awareness of the presence of transcendence all around us, especially as it manifests itself around the edges of existence and at the limits of human experience. Two extreme examples of this can be found in the way that modern society on the one hand deals with death through the phenomenon of the funeral parlour, and on the other hand packages pleasure for our leisure hours.

The Possibility of a new (post-modern) Paradigm

The above social analysis discloses one particular way of looking at reality. As such it raises a number of important questions like what are the underlying assumptions informing this outlook, what are the suppositions supporting this stage of affairs, what is the basic mentality reflected in this contemporary crisis, what kind of paradigm of reality is operative here.

In the course of our analysis we have seen the strong presence of autonomy in science, individualism in society, alienation in politics, and consumerism in culture. Each of these characteristics is the outcome of a particular perception of reality that is by and large atomistic, substantialist, fragmented, and 'objectivist'. Reality is regarded as something that can be carved up into isolated units, independent substances, and unrelated blocks. These divided fragments are simply understood to exist 'out there', given for human exploitation and manipulation without any apparent regard to their interconnectedness. This particular understanding of the world is an amalgam of different philosophical viewpoints: certain forms of Aristotelian substantialism, objectivist ontologies, naïve realism, Cartesian dualism, liberal individualism, and Newtonian mechanisation. These different viewpoints may be reduced to those philosophies that think in terms of the existence of independent substances, and those sciences that approach reality in a rather mechanistic fashion. Their influence on people's lives can be seen in unquestioned assumptions rather than in formally worked-out philosophical or scientific positions. In addition a number of 'alienating dualisms' seem to stem from this particular understanding of reality: nature is divorced from humanity, matter is divided from spirit, body is separated from mind, and subjects stand over objects. These dualisms are responsible for many forms of 'apartness' that exist between nature, humanity and the cosmos.

In contrast and by way of reaction, there is a struggle taking place at present for the birth of a new paradigm concerning our understanding of reality. This birthing of a new paradigm is made up of insights coming together from different sciences: philosophy, the new physics, biology and ecology. Paradigm shifts do not take place overnight. Instead they are the outcome of insights taking place simultaneously in different quarters, insights that slowly but surely coalesce into a new picture of the world. The old paradigm begins to break up and now appears to be no longer viable. The emergence of this new picture of reality is accompanied by a growing awareness that many of the problems in our world are, as we have already seen, fundamentally structural and systemic. This awareness in turn has created the new quest for a global vision of live, a radical desire for unity, and a groping towards human solidarity. There is abroad a passion for oneness in the midst of diversity, a sensing that diversity without unity could be destructive and ultimately chaotic, a pursuit of the whole to which the isolated parts belong.

In broad, general terms the emerging paradigm employs categories like holistic, organic, indivisible, and integrative in its understanding of reality. It is inspired by a process philosophy (A. N. Whitehead and C. Hartshorne), the new physics (F. Capra), a feminist perception of human existence, and an ecological view of life today (J. Cobb). These developments overlap, complement, and nourish each other. Taken together they constitute a post-modern paradigm shift in our understanding of reality today. It would be impossible to adequately summarise these developments here. Yet, some general description of their contours may help us to recognise the shape of the new emerging paradigm of reality.

The father of process philosophy is Alfred North Whitehead. Whitehead's philosophy is outstanding for its strong sense of empiricism coupled with a rigorous form of rationalism. His great achievement has been the critical integration of empiricism and rationalism. His empiricism is thoroughly experiential, and in a manner that goes beyond the narrow empiricism of Hume. For Whitehead 'the starting point . . . is the analytic observation of the components of . . . experience' because 'apart from experience there is nothing'.[7] At the same time the experiential Whitehead sets out rationally 'to frame a coherent, logical, necessary system of general ideas in terms of which every element of our experience can be interpreted'.[8] His generalised interpretation of experience gives rise to an understanding of existence as unified, processive, creative, organic and holistic.

In particular, process philosophy sees the world as one, single reality, made up of organically interrelated entities: 'There is one whole, arising from the interplay of many details.'[9] All of reality is active, relational and processive. This 'philosophy of organism', as Whitehead likes to call it, claims that the universe is not made up of independent substances but closely related energy events: 'the building blocks of the universe, things of which everything else is composed, are energy events'.[10] Within this vision great emphasis is placed on the unity of the world and everything in the world. Primacy is accorded to the causal interconnectedness of 'things' in contrast to their independence. Emphasis is placed on events as distinct from substances, and change becomes as important as permanency. Life is a creative, ongoing organic process living in the reality of God who gently persuades the process forward towards fulfilment into moments of intense experience: 'God is . . . the foundation of order . . . the goad towards novelty.'[11]

This process vision of life finds many parallels in the recent discoveries of the new physics. This of course should come as no surprise since Whitehead openly admits that he came to his philosophical convictions through his studies in mathematical physics.[12] The new physics as initiated by A. Einstein, developed by W. Heisenberg, and refined recently by people like Fritjof Capra[13] has brought about profound changes in our understanding of space and time, cause and effect, and matter. It is now agreed that sub-atomic particles are not solid objects in the way that classical physics suggested. Further, these sub-atomic particles cannot be understood as isolated entities in themselves. Instead these solid seeming objects are more correctly understood as closely interconnected wave-like patterns. Both quantum theory and relativity theory as understood in the new physics bring out the dynamic character of all matter. The recurring and significant themes of the new physics are that the universe is an interconnected web of relations, that this cosmic web of relations is intrinsically dynamic and that the being of matter cannot be separated from its activity.[14] These themes also tell us something about the shape of the new paradigm of reality that is now coming to birth. In perceiving this new paradigm we should remember that the way we understand physics is bound to have some influence on our metaphysics. A physics that talks about static, independent and passive substances will surely give rise to a metaphysics quite different to one informed by a physics that sees 'things' as dynamic, interrelated and active.

Another important index of the emergence of a new paradigm of reality may be taken from the feminist movement. This new movement in the twentieth century is a strong reaction against the dominance of an exclusively male approach to life and the assumption that the male perception of existence is normative for all human beings. In broad terms feminism reacts strongly against the qualities we diagnosed above as characteristic of the modern world. Autonomy, individualism, and domination are typical by-products of a male approach to life and as such do not represent the value perceptions of the other half of the human race or correspond to them. In particular, feminism opposes the many dualisms and dichotomies that we have inherited from our patriarchal past: the sacred and the secular, activity and passivity, reason and emotion, body and soul, material and spiritual, feelings and intellect. Probably the best example is the strong statement that feminism makes concerning the unity that exists between the body and the soul. Here appeal is made specifically to the female experiences of menstruation, intercourse, orgasm, conception, pregnancy, birth, lactation, and menopause, which are indicative of the radical unity that exists between body and soul.[15] These distinctive experiences challenge in a very fundamental way the traditional view that the self is a soul or mind within a body. Equally the experience of pregnancy brings out in a very forceful manner the essential interrelatedness that exists between all human beings. The idea of a separate, isolated, detached self, whether male or female, is an illusion. The self is always part of a larger network of human relationships, not just at birth but throughout life. By overcoming the dichotomy between body and soul, female experiences clearly point towards 'an organic view of the self' and a strong 'sense of the organic unity of distinctive body processes and their harmony and interrelationships'.[16] Feminism also reacts against traditional forms of hierarchy associated with patriarchy. These forms of hierarchy, it is argued, have fostered a false superiority in men which has resulted in perpetuating the inferiority of women in society. In place of these dualisms and hierarchies, feminism affirms a unified, inclusive and integrated approach to reality. Consistent with these principles, feminism at least in its more recent forms does not claim that its perspectives are exclusive to women. Instead all human beings have varying degrees of masculine and feminine qualities, or what the Chinese call Yin and Yang modes of being. To this extent feminism affirms an androgynous approach to human identity.[17] This means that feminism does not seek to overthrow the male perspective by a female perspective as if the truth could be found by replacing one oppression by another oppression. Rather, feminism claims in the first instance to have a viewpoint that is as valid and as worthy of consideration as the viewpoint of the other half of the human race. Once this is established, then feminism seeks to go beyond and transform the traditional female-male polarity into a higher synthesis. Without this movement towards a higher synthesis there is a real danger that the androgynous ideal may continue to reinforce the status quo.[18] The ingredients of that higher synthesis which is our primary concern here are a unified, organic, inclusive and integrative vision of life. The feminist perspective is one that points towards a paradigm of reality which is able to distinguish without separating and separate without dividing and divide without destroying the organic, inclusive and unified character of reality itself.

Closely related to the feminist perspective is the ecological understanding of life. The fundamental thesis of ecology is that the environment is essential to the development of all life, especially human life. The ecological point of view emphasises the life of 'the organism as inseparably inter-connected with its environment'.[19] Thus the ecological model has developed by way of reaction against the evol-utionary outlook, especially that form of evolution which implies that social development can take place at the expense of the environment. Ecology denies that the separate development of the human species is possible without due regard to the rest of the environment. Instead ecology claims that there is an important point of continuity, not identity, between natural and human existence. And yet at the same time ecology acknowledges the superior element of transcendence that belongs to the human in contrast to the purely natural. In particular the ecological model seeks to move beyond a purely mechanistic view of the world. The primary analogue for ecology is the behaviour of a living cell. It is pointed out that the living cell is quite dependent for its development on the environment. In fact, we know that the environment profoundly affects the growth of the living cell. This influence of the environment on the cell is especially evident in the early stages of cellular division. The structure of cell development takes place in dependence on the interconnectedness between the cell and its actual environment. Change the environment and the development of the cell is modified: 'Each element behaves as it does because of the relations it has to other elements in the whole.'[20] The example of the living cell is applied to the larger eco-systems of nature and human existence. This vision of reality calls for greater attention to be given to the harmony and equilibrium that should exist between nature and humanity. Neglect of such harmony will bring its own problems: 'Any serious disturbance will not be limited to a single effect but is likely to spread throughout ... and may even be amplified by its internal feedback.'[21] In effect the ecological model refuses to accept that it is possible to go behind the environment to the existence of independent self-contained entities. Instead the ecological approach stresses that the environment is important to the development of life not only externally but also internally.[22]

Ontological Process and Social Praxis in tandem
What begins to emerge from this conspectus of new approaches to reality is the strong presence of a movement away from objects to relationships, from substances to events, from dualisms to unity, from independence to inter-connectedness, and from individualism to community. The universe begins to appear as one, single, organic reality, made up of interrelated entities which come together in a pro-cessive act of concrescing mutual dependencies and enrich-ments. The world as we experience it is not static, fixed, and pre-determined. Rather it is actively in process of being created and recreated, being dismantled and destroyed, being maintained and repeated, being renewed and trans-formed. This particular paradigm of reality is put forward perhaps most persuasively by the process philosophy of Alfred North Whitehead. This does not mean that we have to buy into everything that Whitehead has written but it does imply that the basic intuitions and insights of Whitehead's philosophy of process appear to provide the most adequate translation of contemporary experience. In this regard it should be remembered that, whatever reservations one may have about Whitehead's system and some of these are quite real,[23] the essence of process philosophy is its availability to ongoing change and revision. Clearly there is a close

relationship between the perspectives of process philosophy and the perspectives of the new physics, feminism and ecology.[24] This emerging new process paradigm of reality has much to offer an effective functioning of social praxis in the future. It is quite clear that the problems facing humanity today are global, structural, and systemic. In view of this, our social analysis and social praxis need to be situated in a conceptual framework for thinking and acting in global, structural and systemic terms. Process philosophy with its emphasis on the organic unity of the world seems best suited to the provision of such a conceptual framework as the underlying supposition in conducting our social analysis and inspiring our social praxis. A piecemeal approach to the problems that beset our world today will no longer succeed at the level of social analysis or praxis. Global problems call for organic and processive perspectives as providing the primary context for social analysis and social praxis. In fact, quite often it is the distinct absence of such a global vision and the neglect of such organic considerations that is responsible for many of our contemporary social and political problems.

What this processive model of reality offers most of all to social praxis is an understanding of reality that is amenable to change and transformation. As Whitehead was fond of reminding his students, the way we think determines the way we act: 'As we think, we live.' The process paradigm of reality brings home the point that the world we live in is not static, fixed and predetermined. Rather, the world is an active, living, processive entity which remains an open and unfinished project.

The ontological character of reality as one of process clearly suggests that it is possible for social praxis to achieve its goal. The aim to change the world through social praxis is not some idle romantic dream; it is rather the heavy responsibility which falls upon the shoulders of a humanity that has become increasingly aware of its own unity, solidarity and social wholeness within a processive view of the world.

Furthermore, it is quite clear that whatever approach one takes to the global problems of our world today there is an overwhelming case to be made in favour of change, as we have already seen in the last chapter, as distinct from maintaining the status quo, especially a status quo which is bedevilled by the social sins of militarism, racism, sexism, and classism. The ills and evils of our world today are as much social as they are individual, structural as much as they are personal, institutional as much as they are private. What is perhaps needed more than anything else in a theology of social praxis is an underlying philosophy which is capable of coping with growth and change at both the individual and social levels. Such a philosophy of change is available in embryo at least in the basic principles of process philosophy. In the light of these points the remaining part of this chapter will try to map out some of the fundamental principles of process philosophy that might inform the work of social praxis.

The first of these principles concerns the question of survival which has come to the fore with frightening force in this century: 'If organisms are to survive then they must work together.'[25] This principle is relevant to such basic issues as the ecological crisis, the North/South polarisation and the East/West nuclear arms race. The basic insight behind this principle is a recognition of the interrelatedness that exists between individuals and society, nations and the global world, organisms and their environment. Where organisms end and the environment begins is not always easy to decide. This fundamental unity between an actuality and its environment requires that there be some kind of effort to enable both aspects of the organic whole to grow together towards some form of mutual enrichment. If this is to happen then there must be, as Whitehead points out, 'the careful provision of the favourable environment for the endurance of the family, the race, or the seed in the fruit'.[26] Without this attention to the organic relationship that exists between the environment and its living organisms, there will surely be conflict, crisis and holocaust.

Closely related to this principle is the following principle of process philosophy:

Any local agitation shakes the whole universe. The distant effects are minute but they are there . . . According to the physics of the present day the environment with its peculiarities seeps into the group agitation which we term matter, and the group agitations extend their character to the environment.[27]

This particular principle is another way of highlighting the organic character of the world in which we live. What happens *here* in one part of the global village has repercussions *there* in another part of the world. This radical unity of the world has been brought home to us quite dramatically in recent times: the invasion of the Falkland Islands, the availability of oil in the Middle East, the extravagance of the the first world, the U.S. decision to site MX missiles in Europe. This global, organic dimension of human existence has been neglected in the past because of the unquestioning acceptance of what Whitehead calls the notion of simple location.[28] The 'fallacy of simple location' implies that matter can exist in a detached, independent self-contained manner without reference to its relation with other regions of space and durations of time. It is assumed that 'a substantial individual "requires nothing but itself in order to exist"'.[29] This kind of outlook is basically an abstraction that fails to take account of the complex network of internal and external relations that belong to all matter. There is a sense in which 'everything is everywhere at all times. For every location involves an aspect of itself in every other location'.[30] As such the notion of simple location is a byproduct of the mechanistic model that characterised seventeenth-century science and became symbolised in the billiard-ball model of reality. The real problem with science then and now was not that it had been too empirical but rather that it had not been empirical enough.[31] For Whitehead every event has a past which becomes part of the present and in turn influences the future. A creative unity is seen to obtain from the past through the present into the future in a way that seeks to avoid the extremes of determinism and arbitrariness. This particular principle of process philosophy alerts social praxis to the complexity of change. The past has a stubbornness about it that must be taken into account in social *praxis* for the future. At the same time this principle reminds the present generation of the enormous responsibility it bears in social praxis for the future. The exploitation of natural resources, not to mention the irrational build-up of nuclear arms, may well deny the next generation a habitable world.

Another principle from process philosophy that is supportive of the aims of social praxis concerns the issue of privatisation:

> The doctrine of minds, as independent substances, leads directly not merely to the private world of experience but also to the private world of morals . . . Accordingly self-respect, and the making the most of your own individual opportunities, together constituted the efficient morality of the leaders among the industrialists of that period [nineteenth century]. The western world is now suffering from the limited moral outlook of the three previous generations.[32]

This tendency towards privatisation exists in opposition to the goals of social praxis. Social praxis aims at generating corporate action whereas privatisation depends on the efforts of the individual and assumes a dichotomy between the private and the public. According to process philosophy this tendency towards privatisation is related to an understanding of the individual as an isolated substance whereas process philosophy sees the human person primarily in organic, relational terms. The source of this distortion is what Whitehead refers to as the fallacy of misplaced concreteness.[33] The most obvious example of misplaced concreteness is to be found in the traditional notions of substance and quality. Here the impression is often given that an entity can be described as a substratum or substance of which certain qualities are predicated. The substratum or substance is independent of external and internal relations. When applied to the human person, the individual is in serious danger of becoming cut off from the wider network of internal and external relations: past history, present experience, family, education, community and environment. For Whitehead, what has happened here is that a high level abstraction, namely substance, has been confused with and taken for a concrete reality.[34] The only concrete realities that exist are relational realities and therefore as such cannot be separated from the larger network of relations. Once again we see that there is no such thing as the private, isolated, detached self. The self is thoroughly social, organic, relational and processive.

By way of reaction against the tendency towards privatisation, Whitehead complains:

> The universe is shivered into a multitude of disconnected substantial things, . . . each exemplifying its private bundle of abstract characters which have found a common home in its own substantial individuality . . . In this way Aristotle's doctrine of Predication and of primary substance have issued into a doctrine of the conjunction of attributes and of the disjunction of primary substances.[35]

In view of this, the tendency towards privatisation with its emphasis on individual well-being to the neglect of social responsibility must be rejected. Equally the corollary of this privatisation, namely that the poor and the oppressed have only themselves to blame for their lot in life and that their condition is the outcome of their own irresponsible choosing and laziness, must be repudiated on the same basis of an organic view of the world. For Whitehead, the source of this privatisation is the philosophy of Descartes which divided the world into bodies and minds, and then went on to suggest that 'a substantial individual "requires nothing but itself in order to exist"'.[36] This emphasis on the independence of the individual was strengthened, according to Whitehead, by Darwin's theory of natural selection and, since the seventeenth century, the description by science of bodies in mechanistic terms.[37] Instead, a relational understanding of reality, especially of the self in contrast to independent privatisation, must replace this tendency towards privatisation and its asocial inclinations. This relational view of the individual undergirds the demands of social praxis and its strong sense of corporate responsibility.

Closely related to Whitehead's explanation of privatisation is his thesis that human action has both a private and public aspect to it: '... every action is at once a private experience and a public utility ...'[38] Whitehead's philosophy of organism attempts to overcome the dichotomy that exists between the private and public aspects of human action. This 'distinction between publicity and privacy is a distinction of reason and is not a distinction between mutually exclusive concrete facts'.[39] Every human action has a public side to it, which he calls 'objective immortality'. Actions give rise to public entities which enter into the constitution of other entities:

> ... the process, or concrescence, of any one actual entity involves the other actual entities among its components. In this way the obvious solidarity of the world receives its explanation.[40]

Human actions become a public part of the 'solidarity of the world' we live in. Such actions create the public conditions that make possible future actions. At the same time human actions have a private aspect to them which Whitehead calls 'the subjective immediacy' of human experience. Actions affect the internal creation of a subject out of the wide range of potentialities that exist in life. The world of different possibilities becomes an actuality through private action: 'The many become one, and are increased by one.'[41] The importance of the private aspect of action lies in the way it brings about the internal constitution of a subject. This composition of the subject as subject is itself value-laden in so far as it now becomes a public fact that will enter into the realisation of other future possibilities. Thus every private action becomes a public fact that will affect the composition of other actualities. This unification of the private and the public aspects of human action provides us with some philosophical foundations for developing a theology of social praxis. Clearly the praxis of Christian faith is never a purely private affair; it always has some public significance which for Christianity finds its ultimate term of reference in advancing or inhibiting the coming of the Kingdom of God.[42]

A theology of social praxis must be guided by the public demands of the Kingdom of God to come. These process perspectives on the nature of human action indicate the impossibility of separating faith and politics, religion and society, God and the world, in working out a theology of social praxis.

A further principle within the emerging process paradigm of reality helps us to correct the cult of individualism which we have already seen as so characteristic of our contemporary situation:

> The foundation of social relations upon individualism and competition was not working well under the new industrial conditions . . . The mere doctrines of freedom, individualism and competition, produced a resurgence of something very like industrial slavery at the base of society.[43]

What Whitehead is reacting against here in the first instance is an unqualified form of individualism and its offshoot of ruthless competitiveness. He is not trying to do away with the importance of the individual *in* society. Instead the individual is always an individual as related to the environment: 'The human being is inseparable from its environment in each occasion of its existence'.[44] In particular Whitehead is unhappy with the nineteenth-century liberal faith which was characterised by the hope that a strong emphasis on individualism would bring about the creation of a happy and harmonious society. This suggestion of absolute individualism has to be qualified by other considerations such as human interdependence, the importance of the environment, the centrality of community, and our relationship with nature. These factors contribute to the character of individuality and prevent any easy isolation of the individual from the restraints as well as opportunities that arise from our belongingness to an organic world. The individual is always an individual in relation to community and environment. Once this fundamental relationship is severed the individual begins to take on an aggressive, exploitive, competitive role towards the larger organic whole of reality. A processive view of the world cannot tolerate or accept the current cult of individual-

ism. Instead the organic vision of life relates the individual
to the larger realities of human existence.

A sixth and final principle from process philosophy that
is helpful for social praxis focuses on the processive identity
of reality itself:

> ... *how* an actual entity *becomes* constitutes what that
> actual entity *is*; so that the two descriptions of an entity
> are not independent. Its 'being' is constituted by its
> 'becoming'. 'This is the principle of process'.[45]

This particular principle lies at the centre of process
philosophy. It highlights how fundamental the action of
becoming is in the constitution of reality and in this way
reminds us once again that reality is not simply an arrange-
ment of private substances in fixed, public places. Reality
is pliable and therefore open to being refashioned; reality as
we experience it today is the outcome of the action of
becoming from the past; reality in the future will be the
result of the present action of becoming.

Our analysis of praxis in the writings of Hegel and Marx
displayed a similar understanding of reality, especially
social reality: an actuality is what it becomes, the individual
is what he or she does. Here we have an extraordinary coming
together of process and praxis insights into a complementary
vision of the primacy of action in life. In particular this principle of process philosophy highlights the influence that
praxis has on the constitution of present and future social
existence. Praxis does shape reality and as such enters into
the composition of reality as we know and experience it
today. Since reality, therefore, is the outcome of praxis then
quite clearly a new praxis is capable of transforming reality.
This means that our praxis must take account of its relational
effect on the environment. Praxis must be guided as much
by the needs of the whole as by the immediate needs of the
individual. There should be no division between individual
praxis and social praxis, between the private domain and
the public realm of transformative praxis, between personal
praxis and historical praxis. A basic unity exists between
becoming and being that challenges the potential of social

praxis for the transformation of the world today. Precisely because the world is in process, the goals of social praxis are now realistically available to us. Once we begin to understand our world as a process of 'being in becoming' then social praxis begins to assume a new and urgent importance in the exercise of all Christian theology.

5

The Church and Christ on Social Praxis

One of the most far-reaching directives to come out of the
Second Vatican Council was the call addressed to the Church
to scrutinise the signs of the times and to interpret them in
the light of the Gospel.[1] By issuing this challenge to the
Church, the Council was proposing a particular way of doing
theology which it felt was more suitable to the kind of world
we live in today. In effect, the Council was suggesting that
theology grows out of the historical experiences of men and
women living in the world. Theology takes place within a
particular context and it is this context which shapes the
content of the Christian agenda. It was the application of this
directive in the post-conciliar period that enabled the
development of praxis-oriented political and liberation
theologies. These developments in theology were accompanied by significant shifts in the Church's formal teaching
which, among other points, we will examine in this chapter.

If we take seriously the task of reading the signs of the
times it must be admitted that a picture of the world emerges
which challenges, in a very radical way, the Christian conscience. We live in a world that is divided unevenly into 'the
haves' and 'the have nots', the rich and the poor, a northern
hemisphere of overproduction and a southern hemisphere of
under-development, a first world of extravagant waste and
a third world of extreme want. These signs of the times are
easily illustrated by some stark statistics: 800 million people
live in a condition of 'absolute poverty';[2] 20 million die of
starvation each year; races of people like the Kampucheans
and Ethiopians are being wiped off the face of the earth
through starvation. Alongside these staggering statistics we

learn that over two hundred thousand million pounds (£200,000,000,000) is spent yearly by the super powers on the arms race. Other disturbing facts and figures could be instanced.

Interpreted in the light of the gospel of Jesus Christ these signs of the times disclose that we live in a situation of sin and injustice which has become institutionalised in our economic, social and political structures. Such a situation is now commonly described as one of 'social sin'. The idea of 'social sin' implies that destructive and dehumanising trends have become built into the basic structures that organise life. Social sin is not normally planned in a deliberate or conscious way; instead it arises indirectly as a consequence of human blindness or personal sin. Nevertheless, 'social sin' is completely contrary to God's plan of creation and salvation. According to the Christian doctrine of creation, the fruits of the earth are intended for the use of every human being and not just to be confined to a powerful, privileged few. Furthermore, this social state of affairs clearly contradicts God's grace of salvation which is offered to all humanity in Christ. In addition this sinful situation inhibits the visible growth of God's Kingdom as present reality and future promise.

The fact that so many people go to bed hungry every night and that millions die of starvation every year is not something divinely preordained. To the contrary, world hunger and world poverty are the by-product of man's mismanagement of human affairs at the economic, social and political level. In particular these global imbalances, and the degradation of human dignity which they bring, are a result of man's inhumanity to humanity. They are a consequence of human sinfulness. Gone are the days when we could exempt ourselves from responsibility for such inequalities by suggesting that they were 'the will of God' and, therefore, that they should be accepted in a spirit of Christian resignation. They are caused, in fact, to a large degree by the will of human beings. This is brought out very clearly by the report *North-South: a Programme for Survival* which, among other things issues an urgent call to global co-operation among all peoples to save the world and its inhabitants from self-destruction before it is too late.[3] It is now generally agreed by social scientists and economic planners that underdevelopment in the third world is related causally to overdevelopment in the first world. We have seen in the last chapter how this view is supported by process philosophy. To this extent those who belong to the first world must bear some responsibility for the situation that exists in the third world.

This outline of the negative signs of the times must be balanced, however, by taking account also of the more positive signs of the times. These include the fact that humanity has at its disposal for the first time the means for reducing many of these unjust situations. The advances of modern science and technology have made it possible to reduce the gross inequalities that exist in the world. Further, it is now clear that humanity is becoming more and more master of its own destiny. Once upon a time, the world controlled humanity. Today humanity controls the world to an ever-increasing degree. Until recently it appeared that man and his world were in the grip of nature and blind historical forces. Now for the first time nature and history are more and more under the control of humanity. The world in the twentieth century has become something of a global village capable of social, political and economic engineering. Creation as we know it is not a closed, finished and fixed system. Instead, our experience points towards the incomplete and unfinished character of creation. It is quite clear that creation is a project and task to be faced collectively by the human race. Today more than ever before we know in the light of the new emerging paradigm of reality discussed in chapter four that what happens in one part of the world has instant repercussions in other parts of the world. In effect, humanity can, if it wishes, reduce in a radical way the causes of world hunger, world poverty, and world injustices. The question is, does humanity have the will to change a world that is presently destined to self-destruction?

This is a new situation brought about by the technical and scientific advances of the twentieth century. These advances have created new possibilities, new responsibilities and new obligations of a magnitude unparalleled in the history of the human race. Without exaggeration it must be acknowledged that civilisation has come to a critical crossroads where fundamental options must be made and basic decisions taken. In the words of Pope John Paul II, 'we have before us here a great drama that can leave nobody indifferent'.[4] The direction of these decisions will determine the character of our world to come. The options taken will decide whether we wish to promote justice or prolong inequality, offer human liberation or perpetuate human oppression. Such is the magnitude of the challenge latent in what we have already referred to as 'the second enlightenment' facing the world today. The spirit of this second enlightenment is captured by Teilhard de Chardin in the following parable:

> Hitherto men have been living at once dispersed and closed in on themselves, like passengers who have met by chance in the hold of a ship without the least idea of its mobile nature or the fact that it is moving. Living, therefore, on the earth that grouped them together, they could think of nothing better to do than quarrel among themselves or try to amuse themselves. And now, by chance, or rather by the normal effect of the passage of time, our eyes have just been opened. The boldest of us have made their way to the deck, and seen the ship that carried us. They have noted the creaming of the bow-waves. They have realized that there are boilers to be fed and a wheel to be manned. Above all, they have seen the clouds above them and smelt the fragrance of the islands over the circle of the horizon. The picture of men ceaselessly in agitation over the same spot has gone; this is no longer an aimless drifting, it is a *passage to be made good*. It is inevitable that some other sort of Mankind must emerge from that vision.[5]

These positive signs of the times have created a new awareness in the secular world at large as well as among the major Churches. On the secular level there is a clarion call to create a new international economic order. New institutions have been set up to deal with these critical issues on a global scale. Such institutions include the different agencies of the United Nations, the International Monetary Fund and Comecon. Further, some governments have now begun to take seriously the world-wide issue of human rights.

Running parallel to these innovations in the secular world has been the existence of significant developments in the Catholic Church's self-understanding of her responsibility to re-make the global village through action for justice. That the Christian community does have a part to play in shaping the world of tomorrow is beyond question. In working out this role the Church has developed a new appreciation of the place of praxis in her mission to the world and in theology at large.

The Teaching of the Church from Vatican II onwards
There can be no doubt that the foundations of this praxis-oriented theology were laid at the Second Vatican Council. These foundations were subsequently developed in a creative way by Pope Paul VI in the seventies, and Pope John Paul II has pledged himself to a continuation of these perspectives in the life of the Church. It is generally agreed that one of the major highlights of the Second Vatican Council was the promulgation of the *Constitution on the Church in the Modern World*. Perhaps the most significant thing about that document is its title. The Church exists *in* the world and as such it exists *for* the world. There is a very real sense in which the world, according to this document, defines the nature of the Church. Prior to the Council there was a tendency to contrast the Church with the world, describing the Church as that perfect society which exists over and against the world. The whole spirit of *Gaudium et Spes* is one which suggests that the Church cannot be fully understood without reference to the world and that if we are to make sense out of the world then we need the light of the Church. Thus the Council states in a very significant sentence that the 'Church is the universal sacrament of salvation for the world'.[6] As such the Church 'is truly and intimately linked with mankind and its history'.[7] Thus there should

be no separation or opposition between the Church and the world. The world is the *locus* of the Church's activity. There should be no dichotomy between Christian commitment and responsibility for the world. The Council, mindful of critiques directed against religion in the past, warns:

They are mistaken who knowing that we have no abiding city seek one which is to come. For they are forgetting that by faith itself they are more than ever obliged to measure up to these duties each according to their proper function ... This split between the faith which many profess and their daily lives deserves to be counted among the more serious errors of our age ... Therefore let there be no false opposition between professional and social activities on the one part and religious life on the other hand.[8]

Already one can begin to see a move in the direction of a new emphasis on the importance of praxis in the thinking of the Church. Belief in the gospel has practical consequences for daily living. This becomes evident when the Council describes the mission of the Church in the world.

The Council sees the mission of the Church as something that is made up of distinct but closely related dimensions. These include the proclamation of the good news of Jesus Christ, the celebration of that good news in word and sacrament and giving concrete witness to the work of Christ in the world. Having affirmed these traditional aspects of the Church's mission the Council then goes on to say that this religious aspect of the Church requires at the same time a practical commitment to the renewal of the temporal sphere. This implies that the Church must be also committed to the creation of a better world,[9] to the promotion of justice,[10] to the development of peoples,[11] and to the defence of human rights.[12] Clearly the Council teaches that the total mission of the Church in the world embraces a religious aspect and a temporal aspect which is directed to the renewal of the secular order.[13] The implications of these ideas were spelt out by Pope Paul VI in a series of significant events in the life of the post-conciliar Church.

The first of these was the appearance of *Fostering the Development of Peoples (Populorum Progressio)* in 1967. In that outstanding encyclical Paul VI begins by issuing a 'solemn appeal for concrete action towards man's complete development and the development of all mankind'.[14] He then goes on to point out that: 'Development demands bold transformations, innovations that go deep. Urgent reforms should be undertaken without delay.'[15] He concludes this extraordinary encyclical: 'The hour for action has now sounded. At stake are the survival of so many . . . the peace of the world and the future of civilization.'[16] In order to practise what he was teaching, Paul VI set up in that same year a Pontifical Commission for Justice and Peace charged 'to further the progress of the poorest peoples, to encourage social justice among nations, to offer to the less developed nations the means whereby they can further their own progress'.[17]

This encyclical was followed by the coming together of the Latin American Episcopal Conference (CELAM) at Medellín, Colombia, 1968. The *Conclusions* of the Medellín Conference encouraged 'the active and receptive, creative and decisive participation (of all) in the construction of a new society'.[18] They also pointed out that 'the present historical moment . . . is characterised by underdevelopment . . . alienation and poverty' which 'awaken attitudes of protest and desire for liberation, development and social justice'.[19] A new Christian confidence, consciousness and courage directed towards action in the name of the gospel was created at this Conference which acted as a catalyst in the construction of liberation theology.

What happened in Latin America began to be felt throughout the universal Church. A new awareness of the importance of action for justice was gathering momentum. In early 1971 Pope Paul VI wrote an apostolic letter, *Octogesima Adveniens*, to Cardinal M. Roy marking the eightieth anniversary of the encyclical *Rerum Novarum* (1891). This important letter addressed itself to the social needs of a changing world. A strong emphasis on collective action for justice prevails throughout[20] and the urgency is highlighted 'to undertake daring and creative innovations which the present state of the world requires'.[21] The letter goes on to state: 'It is not enough to recall principles, state intentions, point to crying injustices, utter prophetic denunciations; these words lack weight unless . . . accompanied . . . by effective action.'[22]

Octogesima Adveniens was followed by the 1971 International Synod of Bishops which continued the discussion about the practical imperatives latent in the gospel. In its final document, *Justice in the World*, the Synod declared in a now famous sentence:

> Action on behalf of justice and participation in the transformation of the world fully appear to us as a constitutive dimension of preaching the gospel, or, in other words, of the Church's mission for the redemption of the human race and its liberation from every oppressive situation.[23]

The same Synod stated that:

> The mission of preaching the gospel dictates . . . that we dedicate ourselves to the liberation of man even in his present existence . . . For unless the Christian message of love and justice shows its effectiveness through action in the world, it will only with difficulty gain credibility with the men of our times.[24]

At the beginning of the 1974 Synod Pope Paul VI returned to the question of the relationship that exists between the gospel and social *praxis*. He reminded the bishops once again that

> There is no separation or opposition, therefore, but a complementary relationship between evangelization and human progress. While distinct and subordinate, one to the other, each calls for the other by reason of their convergence towards the same end: the salvation of man.[25]

While it is true that some words of caution were expressed at that Synod about certain imbalances in liberation theology, the overall thrust of the 1974 Synod positively affirms the existence of an intrinsic relationship between evangelisation and liberation. This can be seen in the two documents

approved and immediately released after the Synod. The
first, *On Human Rights and Reconciliation*, points out that
'the promotion of human rights is required by the Gospel
and is central to her ministry'.[26] The second document,
Evangelisation of the Modern World talks about 'the intimate
connection between evangelisation and liberation' and then
goes on to say that the 'Church, in . . . fulfilling the work of
evangelisation, will announce the total salvation of humans
or rather their complete liberation, and from now on will
start to bring this about'.[27] In his own subsequent reflections
on the 1974 Synod contained in *Evangelisation in the
Modern World* Paul VI asserts the Church's explicit commitment to justice, liberation, development and peace as integral
to evangelisation.[28] In 1977 at a general audience Pope Paul
VI was to take up this theme yet again, reminding his
listeners that:

> There is no doubt that everything which touches human
> promotion, that is the work for justice, development
> and peace in all parts of the world ought also to be an
> integral part of the message . . . Do not separate human
> liberation and salvation in Jesus without however identify-
> ing them.[29]

At this stage it becomes possible to state that there has
emerged within the official teaching of the Catholic Church
a clear theological consensus concerning the integral relatedness of action for justice and the mission of the Church.[30]
The pontificate of Paul VI represents a high watermark in
the Church's self-understanding of her mission in the world
and her commitment to creative action for the sake of social
justice. This is the real legacy of Paul VI to Catholicism in
this century. A clear conscious decision in favour of social
praxis as integral to the gospel was made during the reign of
Paul VI.[31]

We can no longer talk about the religious mission of the
Church as primary and the temporal mission as simply
secondary. Efforts to talk about this socio-temporal aspect
of the mission of the Church in the world, designating
that aspect as improper or substitutional or unofficial

or partial, simply do not take adequate account of the developments, defined above, in the magisterial teaching of the Church.[32] The two distinct aspects, the religious and the socio-temporal, belong intrinsically to one and the same mission of the Church. The religious dimension of the Church's mission is the basis of our commitment to the transformation of the temporary order and our socio-political involvement in the transformation of the world expresses our religious commitment. In effect, we must rid ourselves, therefore, of any artificial conflict that is alleged to exist between the so-called vertical and horizontal dimensions of our Christian faith. We must realise with the 1971 Synod that the horizontal dimension is constitutive of the vertical and that the vertical dimension sustains the horizontal. An underlying unity-within-distinction exists between liberation and salvation, between human progress and evangelisation, between the historical struggle for justice and the coming kingdom of God, and between the temporal mission of the Church and the religious mission of the Church. As such this unity-within-distinction gives rise to a creative and dialectical relationship between the gospel and liberation which enables us to realise that the gospel without liberation is incomplete and liberation without the gospel is unfinished. This intrinsic relationship between transformative action for justice and the gospel of Jesus Christ highlights the creative and dialectical unity that exists between theory and praxis in the whole of theology.

In the early mid seventies some reservations began to appear in different places about this orientation towards social praxis in the life of the Church. As CELAM III drew near, to be held in Puebla, these reservations reappeared and became more vocal. Many of them found their way into the *Preparatory Document* and the *Working Document* drawn up for the Puebla Conference. Concern was stated about the question of violence, the identification of Christianity with ideologies which promise heaven on earth and the use of Marxist analysis in Christian circles.[33] Perhaps the most serious feature about these preliminary documents was the fact that they deliberately set out to offer an alternative to Medellín.[34] This was the kind of atmosphere that preceded the visit of Pope John Paul II to Puebla, Mexico, in January 1979.

The fact that John Paul II decided to go to Puebla is itself significant. In his opening address to the Conference John Paul II did four things. He re-affirmed the importance of Medellín: 'the Conference now opening will have to take the Medellín conclusions as its point of departure'.[35] He called for 'a careful and zealous transmission of the truth about Jesus'.[36] In this connection he corrected certain doctrinal distortions in the areas of Christology[37] and ecclesiology.[38] He re-affirmed explicitly the heritage of Paul VI: 'The Church has learned that an indispensable part of its evangelising mission is made up of work on behalf of justice and human promotion ... that evangelisation and human promotion are linked together by very strong ties of an anthropological, theological, and charitable nature'.[39] Lastly, he pointed out that the Church teaches, 'there is a social mortgage on all private property ... this evangelical principle will lead to a more just and equitable distribution of goods ...'[40] This important address influenced the direction which the Puebla Conference took and this influence is evident in the final document, which is made up of 1,310 propositions.[41] In that final document we find among other things a re-affirmation of the spirit of Medellín, the assertion that there can be no evangelisation without the integral liberation of humanity, a critique of the idols of our time, an option for the poor which is preferential without being exclusive, and a concern for the place of indigenous people in society.[42]

That the Church in Latin America and the Church universal had come to a crossroads at Puebla can hardly be doubted now in retrospect. Pope John Paul II guided the Church steadily through this crossroads in faithful continuity with the insights of Vatican II and the developments of the post-conciliar period of the seventies. Within weeks of his return from Mexico John Paul II took up the theme of liberation theology, in affirmative terms, at one of his general audiences. He asserted that liberation theology is not only for Latin

America; it must also be developed 'on a universal scale'.[43]

A month later there appeared the first encyclical, *Redemptor Hominis*, of John Paul II, which on careful reading should leave no one in doubt as to his commitment to carry through Paul VI's programme of creative action for justice in the world. The key section on this subject is chapter three. Echoing Vatican II, John Paul II says 'the Church must grow through her relationship with Christ reading man's situation in the modern world in accordance with the most important signs of our times' (a.15). As we approach the end of the second millennium these signs of the times disclose 'a time of great progress . . . a time of threat in many forms for man' (a.16). The inequalities that exist between people in the world 'have causes in history' (a.16); they bring 'into question the financial, monetary production and commercial mechanism that . . . support the world economy' (2.16). The elimination of these disorders 'requires daring creative resolves in keeping with man's authentic dignity', the 'resolute commitment by individuals and peoples that are free and linked in solidarity', and 'the indispensable transformation of structures of economic life which will not be easy without the intervention of a true conversion of mind, will and heart' (a.16).

In response to these signs of the times the Pope notes that 'man is the primary route that the Church must travel in fulfilling her mission' (a.14). As a result the Church 'must be aware of all that seems to oppose making "human life ever more human"' (a.14). The overriding horizon of this encyclical, and of chapter three in particular, is the Pope's profound perception of the dignity of man. Whereas *Gaudium et Spes* had described the Church in terms of the world, *Redemptor Hominis* describes the Church in terms of man: 'he is the primary and fundamental way for the Church, the way traced out by Christ himself' (a.14). In the light of this humanity-centred ecclesiology John Paul II can write:

> Inspired by eschatological faith, the Church considers an essential, unbreakably united element of her mission

this solicitude for man, for his humanity, for the future of man on earth and therefore also for the course of development and progress. (a.16)

The same practical concern for the creation of a more just world as something integral to the mission of the Church has been present, in word and deed, throughout the pastoral visits of John Paul II to different countries. For example, in his visit to Brazil in 1980 he points out that: '. . . the Church constantly advocates . . . reforms that aim at a more just society, more and more in conformity with the dignity of the whole person.'[44] Likewise, in his visit to Costa Rica in 1983, he focuses on the social mission of the Church, reminding his audience that: 'This Church . . . exhorts us to be concerned not only with spiritual things, but also with reality of this world and of society of which we are a part.'[45]

Finally, in his encyclical *Laborem Exercens*, John Paul II argues persuasively for the primacy of labour over capital in a language closely related to our treatment of Marx and the critical theorists in chapter two. This relationship is particularly evident in the emphasis given in the encyclical to the primacy of the human subject, the importance of praxis and an action-based understanding of truth,[46] each of which is foundational to a theology of the social mission of the Church in the world today.

Quite clearly and explicitly the present teaching of the Church comes down heavily on the side of social praxis as an integral element in the mission of the Church. The precise nature of this praxis is one of transformation directed towards the integral liberation of people throughout the world who are motivated by the gospel of Jesus Christ. This teaching of the Church is supported by a number of theological reasons which we must now briefly outline.

Christological Grounds for Social Praxis

The mission of the Church derives ultimately from the mission of Jesus Christ. The mission of Christ, from beginning to end, is centred in and directed to the coming Kingdom of God. The Kingdom of God is a complex Jewish

concept which acts as a master-symbol summarising the purpose and goal of the mission of Jesus. Mark begins his gospel
by telling us:

> Jesus came into Gallilee preaching the gospel of God and
> saying: the time is fulfilled, and the Kingdom of God is at
> hand; repent and believe in the gospel.   (Mk. 1:14)

This Kingdom of God preached by Jesus is about the
active healing power and presence of God in the world. This
saving reality of God broke into the world in a new and
creative way through the activity of Jesus. 'But if it is by the
spirit of God that I cast out demons, then the Kingdom of
God has come upon you' (Mt. 12:28). The Kingdom of God
is not some kind of new, private deal between God and the
individual set up by Jesus; rather it is a new collective reality,
brought into being by Jesus, in which the justice of God
reigns supreme. Further, the Kingdom of God is not an
exclusive grouping of people; instead it is an inclusive gathering of people that reaches out in a reconciling manner, like a
net, to those who have been marginalised. Lastly, the
Kingdom of God is not simply some kind of other-worldly,
purely spiritual reality; rather it is the creation of a new
moral order affecting people here and now in their real needs,
governed by the love and justice of God. Through the liberating Spirit of Christ active in the Church and the world at
large this new community of love and justice will only reach
completion with the second coming of Christ. In short, the
Kingdom of God is about the cause of God in the world
today and tomorrow, a divine cause which is centred in the
collective cause of men and women bound together by the
New Covenant making up a New Community of love and
justice.

Entry into the Kingdom of God can only be effected by
way of a radical conversion. This conversion is one that
requires a change at the level of praxis: 'Not everyone who
says to me 'Lord, Lord' shall enter the Kingdom of heaven,
but he who does the will of my Father who is in heaven'
(Mt. 7:21). Belonging to the Kingdom of God and working
for the Kingdom of God, therefore, requires a whole new

style of living and praxis which is directed in service towards the neighbour. This new style of praxis in the Kingdom of God turns the values of this world upside down: it is the poor in spirit that are rich; the peacemakers who are called sons of God; the humbled who are exalted, those who serve who are the greatest, those who mourn that are blessed; you must love not only your friends but also your enemies; if you are asked to go one mile you must go two miles; if you want to enter the Kingdom of God then you must become like little children; and to save your life you must lose it (Mt. 5:3ff; 10:39; 19:14). The parables, which are stories about this new state of affairs, often end with an injunction to act in a new way. In fact the basic structure of most of the parables is the advent of grace which reverses the values of this world and calls for a new form of action: advent, reversal and action.[47] The miracles, many of which are about the healing activity of God in the world operating through the praxis of Jesus, are signs of the coming of God's Kingdom. This new praxis of the Kingdom of God is the source of salvation. Jesus brings this out dramatically in the way he depicts the day of general judgment at the end of time. Only those who have exercised this new praxis to the hungry, the thirsty, the stranger, the naked, the sick, and the imprisoned, will belong to the Kingdom of God in heaven. Thus, the Kingdom of God in its inception and completion (Mt. 11:5; 12:28; 25:31ff.) is associated with this creative praxis, summed up in the great commandment of love of God in love of neighbour.

One of the clearest statements in the New Testament about the praxis of this Kingdom-centred mission of Jesus, and one which at the same time portrays Jesus' own self-understanding of his mission, is to be found in the incident when 'he went up to the synagogue as his custom was, on the Sabbath day' (Lu. 4:16) and there he opened the book of Isaiah where it was written:

> The spirit of the Lord is upon me, because he has anointed me to preach good news to the poor. He sent me to pro-
> claim release to the captives, and recovery of sight to the

blind, to set at liberty those who are oppressed, to proclaim the acceptable year of the Lord.   (Lu. 4:18-19)

This account of the mission of Jesus focuses clearly on the practical and performative character of his mission: a mission directed in the name of the coming Kingdom of God to the transformation of those who are poor, captive, blind, and oppressed, a mission concerned about changing the con-flictual situation of humanity in the world.

It is this new praxis based on the vision of the Kingdom of God which is normative for the Church today. The role of the Church in the world is to be an effective sign and credible sacrament of the Kingdom of God on earth. When Jesus sent the twelve out, he commissioned them to announce the Kingdom of God *and* to witness to this new reality through the activities of healing the sick, raising the dead, and casting out demons (Mt. 10:7-9). The mission of the Church today, therefore, is to continue announcing the Kingdom of God (religious dimension) *and* to work for that Kingdom of God through this new, radical social praxis initiated by Jesus (social dimension). The real purpose and the only purpose of the Church is to serve the Kingdom of God; to sight and signal, to support and celebrate in word and sacrament and action the coming Kingdom of God.

This vision and praxis of Jesus in relation to the Kingdom of God is vindicated by his saving death and resurrection. The resurrection of Jesus from the dead inaugurates and establishes the Kingdom of God. This advent of the Kingdom of God is symbolised in a variety of ways: through the reality of the New Creation in Christ (2 Cor. 5:17), the existence of the First Fruits of God's harvest in the Risen Christ (1 Cor. 15:20), and the promise of the New Heaven and the New Earth (Apoc. 21:1). The key to each of these symbols is the Paschal Mystery of the death and resurrection of Jesus. Each symbol embodies the powerful paradox present in the teaching of Jesus about 'life in death'; death is not the end but the beginning of eternal life. What is done in and for the Kingdom of God assumes new and lasting significance in the light of the resurrection. Praxis in the name of the

Kingdom of God on behalf of the poor and the weak is gathered up into the New Creation through the resurrection. The Resurrection is a statement that injustice, suffering and desolation do not have the last word; in the end it is justice and peace and love that will succeed and triumph through the grace of the Risen Christ. There is a relationship, therefore, between what we do here and now for the Kingdom of God and the final advent of the Kingdom of God at the end of time. Even though this relationship may be one of greater discontinuity than continuity, the eschatological promise that what we do now does bear some affinity to the future Kingdom of God gives praxis a new urgency.

This affinity between social praxis and the coming of God's Kingdom exists on different levels. On the one hand social praxis in the name of Christ and his Church can be a sign of the Kingdom of God. If there were no visible signs of the Kingdom of God on earth, how could we preach and hope for the Kingdom of God in the future? Thus, *Gaudium et Spes* can say that through our work for justice and peace in the world there 'grows the body of a new human family, a body which even now is able to give some kind of fore-shadowing of the new age'[48] to come. Further, those who 'dedicate themselves to the earthly service of men ... make ready the material of the celestial realm'.[49] Lastly, having worked for the values of the Kingdom of God during this life we are assured in the light of the resurrection that 'we will find them again ... freed of stain, burnished and trans-figured'.[50] In other words social praxis undertaken in and for the Kingdom of God will find its purification and perfection in the New Heaven and New Earth to come in virtue of the dynamics of the Paschal Mystery of Jesus. In the words of St Paul everything else will pass away but love and love's labour for the Kingdom of God will last forever in the New Creation (1 Cor. 13:7-8). This does not mean in any sense that human effort can or will bring about the Kingdom of God. The Kingdom of God as present reality is a divine gift and its future realisation comes as absolute grace which goes beyond all human expectations since 'no eye has seen nor ear heard, nor has the heart of man conceived what God has prepared for those who love him' (1 Cor. 2:9). It is this divine bountifulness that stirs up in the human heart a passion to work now for the coming of the Kingdom of God so that we may be ready when the Bridegroom does come. Closely connected with the praxis of the Kingdom of God preached by Jesus, and the Paschal Mystery as the fulfilment of that praxis, is the prophetic tradition of Judaism and of Jesus himself. This tradition strikes a dissonant note throughout the Bible. It makes us feel uncomfortable by reminding us unequivocally that the performance of justice is the basic prerequisite for genuine worship. The prophets of old are frighteningly specific in their emphasis on the primacy of praxis (Amos 5:21ff; Is. 1:13ff.). This strong prophetic tradition of Judaism is taken up by Jesus in his earthly ministry (e.g. Mt. 5:23ff; Mt. 9:13). Worship without practical attention to justice in the Judaeo-Christian tradition is the object of a sharp critical protest. It is this prophetic tradition that also inspires the Church in its turn to adopt a liberating praxis as integral to its mission in the world. We shall return to this important theme in our final chapter.

Another reason justifying praxis as an indispensable element in the gospel of Jesus Christ derives from the very nature of Christian salvation At the heart of the gospel is the good news of salvation in Christ. This good news about salvation is not something simply about the next life. The message of salvation in Christ 'cannot be reduced to a message of hope about death and life following death, however important that good news also is'.[51] Salvation is not exclusively extra-historical and other-worldly: salvation does have some intra-historical bearing on and relationship with life in this world. The gospel announces that the grace of Christ is available here and now in this life, that this grace of Christ heals and transforms present existence, and that this new life of grace enables us to live *now* more fully, no longer as slaves but as sons and in the future as heirs. (Gal. 4:6-7). Equally the grace of Christ inspires us to become more fully human in our dealings with others. Further, this grace of Christ which brings salvation does not come to the individual by way of some kind of vertical immediacy. It is a grace that is mediated in many different ways: through the Church, the sacraments, the scriptures, and praxis which is directed towards the other. Praxis is a fundamental channel of grace in the world both for the recipient and for the doer. This praxis is one of the visible effects of Christ's redemptive presence in the world. And so, praxis is required by those who already share in the redemption of Christ as well as those who are in need of that redemption.

A final reason justifying the importance of social praxis in the mission of the Church today is the new theological awareness of the presence of 'social sin' in the world around us.[52] The doctrine of social sin, which can be found in many recent Church documents,[53] holds that the effects of individual sin can become embodied in different social systems and structures around us. Social sin is a hardening of the consequences of personal sin into the structures of institutions. The existence of these sinful social structures often oppress people, deny basic rights, cause pain and inhibit freedom. One of the purposes of the social mission of the Church is to promote a praxis that is redemptively transformative of these sinful structures.

At the same time we must remember that social sin is the outcome of personal sin and that, therefore, no matter how much the social mission of the Church may succeed we are still faced with the fundamental issue of personal sinfulness. No amount of freedom from unjust social structures will free us from our natural propensity to personal sin. This latter can only be overcome through the gracious forgiveness of God formally available to us in the religious mission of the Church. In this way the religious and social missions of the Church serve each other in the struggle to overcome both individual and social sin.[54]

It is these different theological reasons — namely, the Kingdom-centred mission of Jesus, the Paschal Mystery of Jesus, the Judaeo-Christian prophetic tradition, the nature of Christian salvation, and the new theological awareness of social sin that justify the present praxis orientation of the Church's self-understanding of her social mission in the world today.

Some Consequences of a Praxis-Theology

Accepting the above teaching of the Church on praxis and acknowledging its roots in the mission of Christ for the Kingdom of God, it must be noted that a number of important consequences emerge from this orientation towards praxis. By way of conclusion we will summarise *some* of these consequences. One major consequence of the above discussion is the way we see the role of the Church in the world. The Church, as both Institution and as People, must be committed to change, especially to changing the world as we know it today.[55] As John Paul II pointed out to the workers in Saõ Paulo, Brazil: 'The Church . . . tries to ensure . . . that all aspects of social life where there is injustice should be changed'.[56]

This commitment to changing the world is based on the Church's own understanding of the gospel which she must proclaim and practise. As already noted, the gospel of Jesus Christ contains formal reference to action for justice and peace in the world, practical care and concern for the poor of the world, commitment to the liberation of people, and absolute love for the neighbour. These different elements are not an optional extra in the life of the Christian and the Church. They are, as seen above in our analysis of the teaching of the Church, a constitutive dimension of the gospel. To be committed to these different dimensions of the gospel is to be committed to praxis for change. For this reason the Christian community must be concerned just as much with change as it is with preservation, just as much with mission as it is with maintenance, and just as much with the future as it is with the past. There has been a tendency at times in the life of the Church to settle simply for the latter aspects of the gospel, namely an uncritical maintenance of the past. Such a choice, of course, is the line of least resistance. It is caused by what is sometimes referred to as the presence of 'a softened eschatology'[57] in the life of the Church, that is, an outlook which fails to take seriously the coming Kingdom of God announced by Jesus, the present existence of the New Creation in Christ, and the doctrine of the *parousia*. Speaking as a scientist and a philosopher,

Alfred N. Whitehead was fond of pointing out that 'the pure conservative is fighting against the essence of the universe'.[58] From the Christian point of view we are fighting against the essence of the gospel if our primary concern is simply a repetition of the past. The Gospel of Christ continually challenges us to 'cast off the old' and 'to put on the new' (Ep. 4:22ff.), and to remember that in the end 'the former things will have passed away' (Apoc. 21:4). In this vital sense Christianity is committed to change in the name of the coming of the Kingdom of God. For this reason the Church, in virtue of her mission from Christ, must never appear to identify herself with, or simply promote by inaction, the status quo. Instead, the Church, in fidelity to her mission from the crucified and risen Christ, has a responsibility to be an agent of change (like a leaven) in society for the sake of the coming Kingdom of God.

Arising out of this commitment to change is the need for the Christian and the Church to engage in some form of social analysis. If Christian praxis is to reduce the quantum of hunger, poverty, and injustice in the world then it needs to know the causes for these ills from a social, political and economic point of view. As a general principle we can say that social analysis is related to change for justice in much the same way as diagnosis is related to treatment in regard to health. This is why John Paul II could say to the people of New York gathered in Yankee Stadium: '. . . You will also want to seek out the structural reasons which foster or cause different forms of poverty in the world and in your own country so that you can apply the proper remedies.'[59]

In the light of the last chapter it should be clear that our social analysis must take account of the emerging paradigm of reality as processive, dynamic and organic. Our world, especially the structure of society we live in, is profoundly interdependent, interconnected and interrelated. This organic understanding of human existence will influence the shape of our social analysis. In particular, it will ensure that the social analysis is amenable to the aims of a liberating praxis.

Having made a diagnosis of the structural causes behind

social injustices in the world, the Christian community is in a strong position to do something to advance the Kingdom of God. This will involve, among other things, taking up a prophetic stance in the world on behalf of the poor, deprived, and oppressed. In particular it will necessitate taking sides, standing up, speaking out, and acting on behalf of the under-privileged. This prophetic stance of the Church will be two-edged. It will be made up of a process of denunciation as well as annunciation. The Christian community, in the light of social analysis, will have to denounce and 'call by name every social injustice, discrimination, violence inflicted on man against the body, against the spirit, against his conscience and against his convictions'.[60] At the same time Christian faith will have to announce the basis of its denunciation which is to be found in the absolute dignity of the human person made in the image of God, the equality of all individuals before God, and their oneness in Christ Jesus (Gal. 3:28).

If this commitment to change, social analysis and prophetic witness is to be truly effective then some form of political activity is necessary. Christian faith cannot exempt itself totally from political involvement. Commitment in love and justice to the oppressed of this world is ultimately a political issue. This should be clear in view of the fact that much of the poverty and many of the injustices in the world today are, as we have seen, causally connected to political decisions and structures. At the same time we must acknowledge that the precise relationship between Christian faith and politics is a matter of intense debate and unfinished discussion at present. To that extent we can only touch upon some of the broad principles involved in this rather complex area.

A first set of difficulties that people have with Christian involvement in politics is the danger of political reductionism of the Gospel and/or a neglect of the transcendent dimension of faith. Such difficulties themselves are often based on a misunderstanding of some of the most basic theological principles that belong to the centre of Christianity.

For example, faith does not and cannot exist in isolation, unalloyed from any form of socio-cultural expression and mediation. The transcendence of faith is experienced and expressed only as something immanent in the life of the historical community of faith. Christian faith itself emerges out of the experience of the particular preaching and praxis of Jesus, the miracles and parables of Jesus, and especially the death of Jesus *under Pontius Pilate*, and his resurrection. The universality of Christian faith is embedded in the particularity of the Jesus-event. The Eternal Word of God was Made Flesh at a particular historical moment. This principle of incarnation is essential to Christian faith and its historical embodiment. One of these embodiments is surely political activity. This means that political activity can be an expression, indeed at times an important expression, among others, of Christian faith. As we saw earlier on in chapter one, Gutiérrez singles out the political praxis of liberation as an important 'mediating factor' in communicating the saving mystery of God revealed in Christ Jesus.

Further, the removal of Christian faith from all contact with political activity seems to ignore the fundamental unity-within-difference that exists in Christianity between the human and divine in Jesus (Chalcedon), the intrinsic relation that belongs between reason and faith (Vatican I), and the underlying bond that obtains between nature and grace as well as the Church and the world (Vatican II). In the Gospel of Jesus Christ there is no divorce or dichotomy between faith and life in its many dimensions. The fundamental unity that exists between faith and politics as a basic dimension of life, is a unity-within-distinction: a relationship that requires differentiation without separation. This kind of unity is one that avoids extrinsicism in religion without blurring the existence of distinct though closely related identities.

In addition, it must be pointed out that those who deny that the Gospel of Christ has political implications unwittingly create a vacuum in the social and political world. This vacuum is often filled by realities that are most opposed to the faith that such people are trying to safeguard. In fact, most of the objections against a critical and creative interplay between faith and politics are based on naive forms of religious fideism, supernaturalism, dualism and extrinsicism. What is important, in the end, is that political activity by the Christian be inspired, and be seen to be inspired, by the Gospel of Jesus Christ and not by some alien political ideology.

A second set of difficulties that people have with Christian involvement in politics concerns the complex question about the relationship that should exist between religion and politics. Too many are too much influenced in this regard by the long-standing separation of Church and State. The separation that rightly exists between Church and State must not be allowed to dictate a similar separation between religion and politics.[61] The State is a part of society but it — the State — must not be identified with the totality of human beings that make up society. The State is a juridical entity whereas society is that larger reality made up of the free association of persons existing in a particular geographical area. Neglect of this distinction between State and society has caused some to suggest that there should be a separation between religion and politics. On the one hand the separation of Church and State demands that no government shall try to control religion and that no religion shall try to control government. On the other hand the separation of Church and State does not demand the separation of religion and politics. Failure to grasp the distinction between State and society, and the meaning of the separation of Church and State, lies behind the popular but misplaced slogan that 'religion and politics must be kept apart'. This failure also helps us to understand some of the hysterical reactions to the US Catholic hierarchy in their prophetic stance against nuclear arms.

Indeed the nuclear arms issue is a particularly good example of the kind of interplay that should take place between religion and politics in contrast to the juridical separation that ought to characterise Church and State relations. To silence religion on the nuclear arms question, or indeed on other political issues of public concern, would be to assume that the nuclear arms question, or other public issues, are without ethical and moral significance for society.

Religion would hardly be religion if it had nothing to say about a public issue involving ultimate questions about life and death, especially life and death at the global and cosmic levels. The destructive potential of nuclear power, as the US bishops point out in their pastoral letter on peace, threatens the dignity of the human person, the civilisation we have slowly constructed and even the created order itself.[62] Religion clearly has a responsibility to address itself to political issues of public concern. It should be remembered that the religious community is part of society and therefore has a democratic right to speak from within that society to that society.

Further it must be pointed out that politics is not quite as secular as many would have us believe. A strong case can be made that political questions do have a religious dimension to them when pursued and pushed to their ultimate foundation. Politics cannot avoid dealing with fundamental issues like the dignity and freedom of the individual, the responsible exercise of power and authority, and the possibility of human fulfilment and social destiny. Each of these political issues has a religious dimension to it at base that cannot be ignored. The political arena is by no means devoid of religious significance.[63]

Another way of making the same point about the close relationship that does exist between religion and politics is to observe how in fact they overlap on many points of mutual interest. The religious dimension of human existence does not exist in isolation from the other dimensions of reality: 'it criss-crosses them through its interpretative function and specification of action, reality and the self'.[64] Religion interacts with the social, ethical and political dimension of human existence.

Of course the relation between religion and politics will depend ultimately on how we understand the relationship that exists between revelation and faith, the sacred and the secular, God and humanity. If one opts for an extrinsic relation between God and humanity then quite clearly there is no good reason why religion should have anything to say to the world of politics. If, on the other hand, one decides on an intrinsic relation between God and humanity, as the Christian doctrines of creation and Incarnation seem to suggest, then religion will have something to say to politics. Intrinsicism implies that God is in the world and that world is in God without in any way reducing God to the world or the world to God. Within this perspective God is perceived as that gracious reality that is continuously co-present to humanity in everything humanity does, including the work of politics. There is no area of life that the Christian can a priori decide falls outside the gracious action of God, and so in this case politics cannot and should not be isolated from the religious sphere of life.

A final point confusing the debate about the relation between religion and politics is the privatisation of religion which is still so common. Religion is seen as a purely private affair between God and the individual without having any relationship to the public, social world. We have already seen in the last chapter how unacceptable this dichotomy between the private and the public is within a processive understanding of reality. This tendency towards the privatisation of religion, which was unwittingly promoted by certain strains of existentialist theology, must be rejected for various reasons. For one thing, it seems to suggest that religion is not accountable in the public forum and that, this being the case, some kind of conflict exists between faith and reason. One of the outstanding characteristics of the Catholic tradition has been its emphasis (from Augustine through Aquinas to the first Vatican Council) on the intellectual credibility of Christian faith. Faith and reason are seen to complement and enrich each other. This important tradition is presently being recovered in the creative work of David Tracy who sees theology as a discipline that is accountable to three different publics: the Church, the academy, and society.[65] Without attention to accountability in public, especially the publics of the academy and society, theology and religion are in danger of appearing superstitious. By being public and accountable, theology and religion will automatically have something to say to politics. On the other hand, the privatisation of religion leaves, as we have already noted, a vacuum in politics. This vacuum is vulnerable to the creation of dangerous ideologies and strange idolatries in politics. In a word, religion without contact with the world of politics becomes narcissistic, and politics without a religious dimension becomes demonic.

This means, in effect, that Christian faith cannot exempt itself from some form of political involvement and at the same time claim that commitment to social justice is at the centre of the gospel. To remain politically neutral is to run the risk of promoting the status quo and thereby maintaining the structures that cause poverty to continue in existence. To do nothing is to do something; it is to acquiesce in the structures that permit the poor to become poorer and the rich to become richer. This was the reason that the Second Vatican Council urged people 'to remember the saying of the Fathers "feed the man dying of hunger, because if you do not feed him you have killed him".'[66]

The nature of this political involvement by Christian faith should be one of protest and this protest should be largely negative in character. The political involvement of Christian faith should be one of protest against the present social, political and economic structures that cause injustices. This protest must, of its nature, be mainly negative because faith does not have any specific competence in the area of politics[67] nor does it have at its disposal any particular blueprint on the social, economic and political issues of our day.[68] Rather, Christian faith takes full account of the fact that there is no such thing as the perfect social order. Therefore, Christian faith must be critical of both right-wing and left-wing political structures. Neither capitalism nor socialism nor any other political '-ism' can effect the Kingdom of God on earth. To this extent Christian faith exercises a reserve, an eschatological reserve, towards every political system, seeing it as a means and a step on the way to the realisation of God's Kingdom which comes at the end of time as absolute gift. Thus every Christian effort towards the creation of a better world is preparatory, provisional and penultimate to the final coming of God's Kingdom. At the same time, however, it must be acknowledged that negative protest and eschatological reserve is not enough. Christian faith does have within itself positive resources to draw upon. These include the embryonic redemption of the world as given in Christ. The saving grace of God revealed in Christ enables Christian faith to bring to the world of politics a particular perspective on social and historical existence that would otherwise be absent. This particular perspective includes the gift of salvation offered to all in Christ: the Resurrection of the dead, the promise of a new Creation, the hope of a New Heaven and New Earth, and the gracious coming of God's Kingdom. More than ever before, there is a need for Christian faith to exercise its redemptive imagination in political activity. Christian faith is at present in search of new images that are appropriate to the redemptive and eschatological message of the biblical tradition: liberation, fulfilment, a new humanity, the unity of diverse cultures, a world community, and cosmic peace. The adequacy of these images will be judged by their ability to generate a liberating social praxis. Without this capacity to evoke an emancipatory praxis, these new images will appear at best suspect and at worst ideological.

It is precisely this positive perspective of Christian faith in relation to politics that Pope Paul VI was hinting at in his call for a 'rebirth of utopias'[69] to overcome bureaucratic socialism, technocratic capitalism and authoritarian democracy. Such a 'rebirth of utopias', he points out: 'often provokes the forward looking imagination both to perceive in the present the disregarded possibility hidden within it, and to direct itself towards a fresh future.'[70]

In this sense it must be said that Christian faith has within itself both negative and positive resources that can be brought to bear on political issues. Indeed the negative protest of faith is born out of its positive affirmations about the grace and offer of salvation to all in Christ.

The principal challenge facing Christianity today, as we have seen throughout these pages, is not one of doctrine and belief but one of practical witness and liberating praxis that adequately reflects the claims of orthodoxy. The only truly effective and credible Christian answer to the perennial questions about evil, poverty and injustice in our world today is to do something about removing them. Anything short of a liberating action is mere theory and can hardly be said to belong to the centre of Christian faith.

While we have spent much time emphasising the critical relationship that should exist between politics and religion, we must also point out that Christianity cannot become identified with any one particular political party or theory. The political power of Christian faith derives paradoxically from its refusal to adopt any one particular political system. It is precisely this critical reserve of Christian faith towards all particular political positions that enables the Christian message to be a liberating leaven in the world of politics. Equally it should be remembered that all praxis undertaken for the sake of justice and in the name of the Kingdom of God is restricted by the inner sinfulness of humanity which God and only God can overcome through the abundance of his forgiving love and reconciling grace that has drawn near to us in Christ Jesus. This should not deter us, however, from struggling in praxis to overcome the social, political and economic consequences of this sinfulness.

It should be noted here that our observations about political involvement have been directed to individual Christian faith and its exercise in small Christian communities. The question arises, however, as to where the official Church stands in regard to political involvement. Most commentators make a distinction here between the Church as People of God and the Church as hierarchy-institution. Within this distinction it is held that the Church as a People should become involved in the political realm, whereas it is the Church as hierarchy that should animate this involvement of the people. Thus it is argued that the hierarchical Church should not become involved or identified, in normal circumstances, with party politics. This would seem to be the mind of John Paul II in his recent addresses to priests during papal journeys, addresses which have exhorted them to avoid party politics. This also appears to be the case with the Vatican departments that have requested individual priests like the Reverend Robert Drinan SJ, and others involved in party politics, to withdraw from such involvement. The purpose of this distancing of the Church as institution from party politics is to avoid the danger of giving the impression that the official Church favours any one political system and to avoid confusing the Gospel with particular political ideologies. By being non-political the institutional Church will have the strongest possible political influence in the world at large. It will be able to speak out and act against injustices in a way that no particular political party platform could facilitate. When the institutional Church does act in this way the primary focus of interest in her call to a transforming praxis will be the Gospel of Jesus Christ as centred in the dignity of the person and the Kingdom of God.

While this particular position does seem to make sense in theory, it must be acknowledged that in practice it contains a number of unresolved tensions. For one thing, the division of the Church into hierarchy and People is not sufficiently grounded in the ecclesiology of the Second Vatican Council which, in the first instance, emphasises the fundamental unity of all the members of the one Body of Christ. Do not the bishops, as members of the people of God, also have a social mission that cannot simply be confined to the laity? Is it not true to say that their witness extends beyond that of simply animating the Christian community? Is not the US Bishops' stance against nuclear arms a good example of such witness on a public issue before the whole world? In distinguishing between the religious and social mission of the Church in the world we must be careful not to separate. Likewise in allocating responsibilities we must avoid making distinctions that go against the fundamental unity of the whole Christian community 'in Christ', especially distinctions that unthinkingly promote a clericalised mentality of 'them and us'.

Whether, in fact, Christian faith can effectively execute its moral responsibilities in the socio-political realm without contact with party politics is a matter that will continue to command discussion. It does seem strange at times that a Church which can be so sure-footed about the place of certain moral issues in the political arena can, at the same time, be so shy about political involvement when it comes to social praxis in the name of justice on behalf of the poor and oppressed.

This review of the rise of a praxis-oriented theology in the teaching of the Church and Christ has far-reaching implications. Suffice it to say that it provides us with new foundations for the performance of a social theology that could change the quality of life for all and renew the face of the Church in the years ahead. This turn to praxis will enable Christianity to overcome the anomaly of theory without practice and practice without theory that we spoke about in our opening chapter. Further, this emphasis on the primacy of praxis should stir the conscience of the Christian community to become involved, in a spirit of liberating change, with the burning social, political and economic issues facing the world at this critical juncture in its history. Only in this way will Marx's critique of religion lose its fascination for so many people. In addition, this call to a transforming social praxis by the Church will lead to a much needed deprivatisation of Christian faith. Most of all a *praxis*-oriented theology will rid Christianity of that constant danger of sacralising the status quo and taking refuge in new forms of Gnosticism.

6

The Eucharist and the Praxis of Social Justice

We have seen in previous chapters how the turn to praxis in political and liberation theologies calls for new philosophical principles. We have indicated the broad direction of these principles in terms of epistemology and anthropology. We have also seen how social praxis presupposes a more unified vision of reality and how this vision might be developed through some form of the organic perspectives of process philosophy. Further, we have indicated some of the social and political implications of the turn to praxis for Christian faith today. Lastly, we have outlined how the Church has formally recognised the essential importance of social praxis in the proclamation of the Gospel and how this gives rise to a new perception of the mission of the Church in the world today.

In this concluding chapter we will show how orthodoxy and orthopraxis belong together in a creative tension. We will do this with particular reference to the celebration of the eucharist. The purpose of this chapter is to show in the light of what has emerged in previous chapters, how the doctrine of the eucharist (orthodoxy) is intrinsically related to a liberating action for social justice (orthopraxis). We will begin our reflection with a short statement of the problem concerning the eucharist today and this will be followed by an examination of the Judaeo-Christian prophetic tradition in regard to worship. We will then look at the contemporary developments in our understanding of the eucharist and conclude with an analysis of Paul's theology of the eucharist in his first letter to the Corinthians.

A Statement of the Problem

The theology of the eucharist in the past has been characterised to a large degree by a concern for orthodoxy. We are all familiar with the extensive debates that were carried on in the Middle Ages, during the Reformation and the Counter-Reformation periods concerning the real presence of Christ in the eucharist. These debates have continued right up to the twentieth century. Indeed, theories about transubstantiation, transfinalisation, and transignification abound to the present day. Another equally important discussion, sparked off by the Second Vatican Council and some subsequent agreed statements on the eucharist, concerns the nature of the eucharist as a meal in contrast to the more traditional Catholic doctrine of the eucharist as sacrifice. These debates and the doctrinal definitions which they have generated are important for a proper appreciation of the eucharist. They help to safeguard the fullness of the eucharistic mystery. At the same time, however, they can distract us from other equally important dimensions of the eucharist. One of these is the close relationship that exists between celebration of the eucharist and action for justice in the world.

The basic thesis that we wish to put forward in this final chapter might be summarised in the following way. There is an essential link between the liturgy and life, between the sacrifice of the Mass and social justice, between the celebration of the eucharist by the Church and the mission of the Church in the world for the kingdom of God. The authentic celebration of the eucharist requires some form of social action for justice by the community, directed towards the values of the kingdom of God. The eucharistic community should be a force in the world for the transformation of society. In so far as this liberating action for justice is absent from the Mass, to that extent we have to say that an essential element of the eucharistic mystery is missing. This thesis that Christian action for justice is bound up with the celebration of the eucharist is as important as the other basic doctrines of the eucharist such as the real presence, the sacrifice of Calvary, the paschal meal, and the memorial.

Put in a slightly different way we could say that in our theology of the eucharist we have gained orthodoxy at the expense of orthopraxis. We have succeeded in defending right theories about the eucharist while being somewhat less successful in promoting the right praxis. All of us are familiar with the observation that there is a glaring gap between Sunday attendance at Mass and the actual practice of social justice in daily living.

Because of this divorce between the celebration of the eucharist and the social praxis of justice, it is not uncommon to find Christians fully committed to the creation of a better world for the sake of the kingdom of God, who have at the same time opted out of the eucharistic community. There is a growing number of people today passionately concerned about the issues of justice and peace in the world, who have written off as 'irrelevant' the Sunday liturgy. For them the Mass seems to endorse the status quo, to induce a form of social indifference and at times to promote a private type of religion. The Sunday liturgy appears to bear no practical relationship to the burning social questions of the day: the denial of human rights, injustice, unemployment, poverty, discrimination, social inequality, and threat of nuclear destruction.

Indeeed it has been noted by more than one commentator that totalitarian regimes that are unfriendly to the Church usually 'begin by forbidding Christians any form of self-organised action in society, they then prohibit or supervise religious instruction and preaching; but in general they allow worship as inoffensive. Moreover, they sometimes consider the liturgy to be useful because it inculcates respect for the ruling order and submission to the established order'.[1] Another equally disturbing feature of some forms of contemporary liturgy is the way they have begun to assume a very functional role. Within this perspective, liturgy provides something of 'a break' from the hurly-burly of daily life and 'an escape' from the social responsibilities we bear for the world around us. Liturgy sometimes seems to function as a *fuga mundi*, a flight from the world, removing us temporarily from the stark realities of evil and suffering, oppression, alienation and estrangement, within which most mortals have to live out their daily existence.[2]

By way of response to this serious pastoral problem we would like to suggest that the primary function of liturgy is not to endorse the political status quo or reinforce the reigning social ideology. To the contrary, liturgy must be understood as an important source for the creation of new life, opening up new possibilities for the future in the light of God's covenant with humanity established in the saving death and resurrection of Jesus. Liturgy as such provides a context in which the prophetic word of God and the liberating feast of the eucharist interact with the world of suffering, estrangement and social sin. The liturgy is that forum in which religion and politics, God and society, Christian faith and social praxis creatively interact with one another. It is only when this begins to happen that the primary purpose of liturgy which is to give thanks and praise to the glory of God is realised. This offering of thanks and praise to God must include reference to the redemption of the world in Christ which, as we have seen, is both gift and task, reality and promise, affecting the here and now of historical existence. To the extent that the liturgy fails to transform the present in terms of a praxis that is liberating and a process that involves us socially in the lives of others, it fails to be a specifically Christian form of liturgy. Christian liturgy must take account of humanity's needs of salvation and the vistas opened up on how to meet those needs in the story of Jesus.

In particular we wish to suggest in this final chapter that an essential element in the celebration of the eucharist should be raising the consciousness of those who worship to their responsibility for effecting a liberating change in the world around us and the creation of a more just society in the service of the kingdom of God. The authentic celebration of the eucharist should inspire some form of action for justice in the world, and genuine action for justice in the world must be rooted in the paschal dynamics of the eucharist community. Participation in the eucharistic mystery carries with it a serious obligation to share with others. A fundamental link exists between the work of justice and the celebration of the eucharist. This link can be seen to exist on several different levels: critical, creative and sustaining.

It is critical in so far as the unity of all 'in Christ' celebrated in the eucharist reminds us in a powerful way of how far short we have fallen of this reality in daily living. The unity among people brought about by the eucharist is a prophetic critique of the prevailing social conditions of disunity, injustice, inequality and the discrimination that takes place in society.

The link between the eucharist and justice is creative in the sense that the experience of communion 'in Christ' effected by the eucharist animates and motivates the community to work towards the universal sisterhood-brotherhood of humanity in the world. In this sense the eucharist can become a creative instrument for the integral liberation of men and women in the world. The encounter with Christ in the eucharist stirs up the imagination to work towards a justice based on peace that is 'rich in mercy' and rooted in Christian love. The eucharist changes society by first of all changing the inner self of the participants who encounter Christ in the breaking of the bread.

Thirdly, the link between the eucharist and justice is one that is mutually sustaining. The work of social justice needs a goal if it is to be viable. That goal is given in the eucharist which provides us with a foretaste of the heavenly banquet to come. The eucharistic community which is both a sign and a sacrament of the kingdom of God provides an important orientation to all action for justice in the world. At the same time celebration of the eucharist should be related to the needs of the community. These needs, which are ultimately redemptive needs, are especially evident today in the realms of human rights, justice, peace, equality and love.

This particular relationship between the eucharist and justice that we are suggesting here is by no means original. There has always been some connection between the celebration of the eucharist and concern for justice in the world within the Christian tradition. However, it can be said without exaggeration that this link between the eucharist and justice has not always been evident in the life of the Christian community. Further, it seems true to say that this important bond between the eucharist and justice has been neglected in the liturgical renewal generated by the Second Vatican Council. This renewal at times has fallen prey to the demands of a consumerist society: throw-away missalettes, the forty-five minutes in and out turnover of people on Sunday, and the provision of a functional release from secular stresses. Such consumerism has no time for a liberating creativity, aesthetics, activity for justice, prophetic discord or imaginative dissonance — all of which belong to the inner dynamics of Christian liturgy.

The need to bring out the intrinsic connection between the eucharist and social justice is particularly urgent at this historical moment when our world is becoming increasingly fragile, fragmented and threatened from an economic and social and political and nuclear point of view. Not only that but the future of the liturgical movement, especially in terms of the eucharist, will depend in large measure on the extent to which it can successfully forge a liberating social *praxis* that is critically and creatively informed by the celebration of the eucharist. The Church today is faced with a new generation of young people who are firmly committed to justice in the world but fail to see what they call 'the relevancy' of the Sunday eucharist to this commitment.

The Judaeo-Christian Prophetic Tradition

To bring about a recovery of this link between the eucharist and social justice we need first of all to look at the resources available to us from within the Christian tradition. Probably the most potent resource for the basic thesis of this concluding chapter is the powerful prophetic tradition of the Bible. This tradition explicitly condemns worship without justice. Within Judaism the prophets of the Old Testament are especially critical of worship that ignores justice. They consistently condemn worship that neglects the need of justice in the community. Amos, writing in the eighth century B.C. points out:

The Lord says,
'I hate your religious festivals.
I cannot stand them.
When you bring your burnt offerings
     and grain offerings
I will not accept them.
Stop your noisy songs,
I do not want to listen to your harps.
Instead let justice flow like a stream
And righteousness like a river that
     never goes dry.'   (Amos 5:21–25)

In an equally outspoken manner the prophet Isaiah has this to say:

I am disgusted with the smell
     of incense you burn
Your sabbaths, and your religious
     gatherings.
They are all corrupted by your sins.
Yes, stop doing evil
     and learn to do right.
See that justice is done.
Help those who are oppressed.
Give orphans their rights
     and defend widows.   (I. 1:13ff.)

In a similar spirit, the Book of Isaiah can say later on in a discussion about worship centred around the notion of fasting that justice and concern for the poor are essential to the way we worship. The people of God are angry because they have fasted and God does not appear to be impressed. God responds through the prophet Isaiah that their fasting has only made them quarrel among themselves and oppress their fellow human beings. This is not the kind of fasting, or worship, that God wants. The appropriate alternative is then outlined:

The Lord says to them,
'The truth is that at the same
     time as you fast

You pursue your interests and
   oppress your workers.
The kind of fasting I want
   is this:
Remove the chains of oppression,
   and the yoke of injustice,
And let the oppressed go free.
Share your food with the hungry,
And open your homes to the
   homeless poor.
Give clothes to those who have
   nothing to wear,
And do not refuse to help your
   own relatives.'   (I. 58:3ff)

This prophetic tradition is taken up by Jesus who consciously identifies with it during his ministry. He refers explicitly to it in one of his many discordant discourses with the Pharisees. He appeals to them:

Go and learn what this means.
'I desire mercy, and not sacrifice.'

          (Mt. 9:13; cf. Hos. 6:6)

On another occasion Jesus instructs his disciples that:

If you are offering your gift
   at the altar
And there remember that your brother
   has something against you,
Leave your gift, first be reconciled,
And then offer your gift.

          (Mt. 25:23—24)

Worship without practical attention to justice in the Judeao-Christian tradition is, therefore, the object of a sharp critical protest.

   Equally significant in the ministry of Jesus is the washing of the disciples' feet which brings out dramatically the relationship that exists between the eucharist and the liberating service of others. This particular prophetic act is recorded only in John's gospel (Jn. 18:1–20). It appears in that part of the fourth gospel where we would expect to find the narrative account of the institution of the eucharist. Commentators hold that this replacement of the institution of the eucharist by the foot-washing incident is deliberate by John. It is John's way of trying to bring out the connection between the eucharist and service of others. In replacing the liturgical act of the eucharist with the washing of the feet, John is here substituting for the sacrament the reality that it signifies, namely the active service of others in charity.[3]

Further it is suggested that the washing of the feet is an 'analogue of the institution narrative in the synoptic accounts of the supper'.[4] The washing of the feet by Jesus is, therefore, an explanation of what the eucharist is really all about; it is a symbolic commentary on the deeper meaning of the eucharist provided by Jesus; it reveals Jesus as the servant who gives his life in the service of others.

What is perhaps even more significant is that John concludes his account of the washing of the disciples' feet with the command 'that you also should do what I have done for you' (Jn. 13:15), a command that parallels the eucharistic command, 'Do this in memory of me.' Also instructive here is the fact that John finishes this particular chapter of his gospel by recalling the great commandment within the context of this dramatic and symbolic act of washing the feet of his disciples.

A new commandment I give to you,
That you love one another;
Even as I have loved you,
That you also love one another.
By this all men will know
That you are my disciples,
If you have love for one another.

(Jn. 13:34–5)

This interpretation of the foot-washing incident in John's gospel in terms of linking worship with service is justified on two other different counts. On the one hand Jesus had already identified himself with the Judaeo-prophetic

tradition which condemned worship without justice. Clearly
he would have wished to bring out dramatically this connection between worship and justice, between the institution
of the eucharist and its relationship to the service of others.
On the other hand, the liturgy of the Church on Holy
Thursday which recalls the institution of the eucharist
includes the foot-washing incident at least as an option. In
this way a bond between the eucharist and service is retained
at least in ritual form in our liturgical tradition.

Furthermore, the practice of the early Church as portrayed
in the Acts of the Apostles shows that there was a real
concern for the poor in the context of the eucharistic breaking of the bread:

> And they devoted themselves to the
>   apostles' teaching and fellowship,
> To the breaking of bread and the
>   prayers . . .
> And all who believed were together
> And had all things in common;
> And they sold their possessions and goods,
> And distributed them to all as had any
>   need.
>
> (Acts 2:42, 44, 45)

The same kind of concern is found in the writings of St Paul,
especially in his first letter to the Corinthians which we shall
presently examine. It seems clear that in the first century
a collection was taken up during the celebration of the
eucharist and distributed to the poor and needy. There is
evidence among the early Fathers, such as Justin Martyr and
Polycarp, that this custom of taking up a collection and dis-
tributing it among the poor was continued at least up to the
third century.

The point emerging from this rapid review of the biblical
tradition is that an indissoluble link exists between worship
and social justice. This link is specified in early Christianity
through the explicit association of the eucharist with the
service of others, especially the poor. The need to integrate
liturgy and social action is brought out dramatically in a

homily by St John Chrysostom, Bishop of Constantinople, around the year 400 A.D :

> Do you want to honour Christ's Body? Then do not honour him here in the Church with silken garments while neglecting him outside where he is cold and naked . . . Of what use is it to weigh down Christ's table with golden cups when he himself is dying of hunger? First fill him when he is hungry; then use the means you have left to adorn his table.[5]

Contemporary Understanding of the Eucharist

Moving from the early Church to the contemporary situation, we have already seen how the Catholic Church in the latter half of this century has made a deliberate and conscious decision in favour of action for justice as an integral element of her mission in the world.[6] This development is so significant that one could say that the Church is still only coming to grips with the full social implications of this important decision. The turning to experience, the human subject and social praxis, and their advent into the outlook and language and practice of the Catholic Church will take time to fully unravel. One particular area in which the perspectives of political theology, liberation theology and social theology have yet to be fully applied is the liturgy of the eucharist. For example, we say that 'the eucharist makes the Church' and that 'the Church makes the eucharist'. If, however, the Church's self-understanding embodies a fundamental commitment to action for justice, then the eucharist is one way of critically and creatively effecting a praxis of Christian liberation in the world today.

Already traces of this development are beginning to appear in our contemporary understanding of the eucharist. A good example of this can be found in the agreed statement on the eucharist between Catholics and Protestants in France, known as *Les Dombes* statement issued in 1972. It has this to say:

> Reconciled in the eucharist, the members of the Body of Christ become the servants of reconciliation among men

and witness to the joy of the resurrection ... The celebration of the eucharist, the breaking of bread that is
necessary to life, is an incitement not to accept the conditions in which men are deprived of bread, justice and
peace.[7]

Again, in another section of the same document under the
heading 'The Eucharist: A force for the liberation of Mankind' we read:

We accept his [Christ's] invitation to his table, we are
taking up his mission in his footsteps by our witness of
faith and hope, by our fight against the forces of oppression,
destruction and death, in order to reconcile all things and
and offer everything to God.[8]

A further example of this may be found in the Lenten
Address of John Paul II on *The Holy Eucharist* which takes
up this particular theme.[9] He speaks of the eucharist as 'the
active school of love for neighbour' (a.6). He then goes on
to note that if our eucharistic worship is authentic then
it will make us grow in awareness of the dignity of each
person and that in turn will make us 'particularly sensitive
to all human suffering and misery, to all injustices and
wrong, and seek the way to redress them effectively.' (a.6).

This re-emerging insight from the relationship between the
eucharist and social justice was given formal recognition by
the 42nd International Eucharistic Congress held in 1981
at Lourdes.[10] The theme of that Eucharistic Congress was
'Jesus Christ bread broken for a new world'.[11] The choice
of words and the images evoked in this title are particularly
significant for a contemporary understanding of the eucharist.
The title of the Congress brings together in a formal way the
creative unity that obtains between the breaking of the
eucharistic bread and the Christian commitment to the
creation of a new world. When this theme was chosen John
Paul II wrote an important letter to Cardinal Knox, the
President of the Permanent Committee for Eucharistic
Congresses. In that letter the Pope provides particular
'orientations' that reflection on the eucharist might take
during the Congress. He points out that the creation of a

new world is one of the principal fruits of the celebration of the eucharist. This new world is one 'marked by filial relations with God and fraternal relations with people'.[12] For John Paul II the breaking of the bread by the Church in the name of Christ 'has great consequences for society'. These include:

Bringing people together in
    fraternal unity,
especially the poor.
Scrving them,
sharing with them the bread of
    the earth
and the bread of love,
building up with them a more
    just world,
preparing a new world for the
    future . . . [13]

In particular John Paul II called upon the Congress 'to deepen and to express to people of today how and why the new world is linked with the eucharist'.[14] He also suggested that the Congress should bring out the 'ethical dynamism the eucharistic Christ imparts to those who feed upon him'.[15] An adequate response as to how these recommendations might be met today is clearly beyond the scope of this chapter. At the same time, however, it may be useful to suggest the general direction that such a response might take.

Concerning the link between the new world and the eucharist we have already seen something of the biblical basis for this within the Judaeo-Christian prophetic tradition and also how this is presently being recovered in the Church's new consciousness of her mission in the world today. It may be helpful to add to that some further reflections on how the basic doctrines of the eucharist, like the real presence, sacrifice, meal and memorial do in fact demand a liberating praxis for the creation of a new world. Before doing this we should be clear as to what is meant by the phrase 'new world' in the title of the Eucharistic Congress. The new world is the Kingdom of God announced and promised by the earthly Jesus, gained and brought into being by his saving death on the cross, manifested in the glory of his resurrection and inaugurated by the outpouring of the Holy Spirit. This new world which is already established in the Body of the risen Christ will reach completion and final perfection in the fullness of time when Christ will unite all things in heaven and on earth (Ep. 1:9—10). In the meantime, this new world exists in embryonic form wherever and whenever the values of the Kingdom of God are promoted by a liberating action in the service of the cause of humanity. The transformation of human existence, history and the universe, in the name of the Kingdom of God gives us 'some foreshadowing of the new age' to come.[16]

The doctrine of the real presence of Christ in the eucharist is related, as Paul VI pointed out in *Mysterium Fidei*, to the many presences of Christ in the world: the presence of Christ in the eucharist, in the word of God, in the minister, and in the congregation. The real presence of Christ in the eucharist is a sacramental realisation of that general presence of Christ in the Christian community and throughout the world. Above all the real presence of Christ in the eucharist is the presence of the Risen Christ in whom the new world has already begun. The sacramental presence of Christ in the eucharist is brought about by the proclamation of the word of God, the invocation of the spirit, and the recitation of the canon of the Mass by the ordained minister. This real presence of Christ in the eucharist is a presence with a purpose: that they may be one, that they may have life and have it more abundantly, that they may eat and not die (Jn. 6:50). As such the real presence of Christ in the eucharistic community is pure gift offered to humanity for the saving purposes of healing, reconciling, liberating and unifying all 'in Christ'. This particular saving purpose of the eucharist is one that brings about the creation of a new world. At the same time it must be remembered that this Christ who is really, truly and 'substantially' present in the eucharist is the same Christ who is also personally present in the poor and downtrodden of this world. These two presences of Christ must be kept together and understood as complementing each other. We cannot consistently choose the comfortable real presence of Christ in the eucharist and ignore the disturbing personal presence of Christ in the poor and the downtrodden. Commitment to Christ in the eucharist carries with it a commitment to Christ in the poor of this world. In this way an indissoluble relationship exists between the celebration of the eucharist and the creation of a better world.

The mystery of the eucharist is also about the sacrifice of Christ on the cross of Calvary. In the eucharist we renew the one and only sacrifice of Christ. This renewal is a powerful call to each one of us to share in a personal way in the sacrifice of the cross. The objective salvation brought about by the sacrifice of Christ must be assimilated subjectively by his people on earth. As followers of Christ we must pass over from sin to grace, from darkness to light, from slavery to freedom, and from death to life. That passover takes place in the sacrifice of the Mass. It requires in each one of us a personal and communal conversion. The sacrifice of the Mass leads to conversion, a change in life-style, a passover to the values of the kingdom of God: universal justice, peace and love. This conversion requires at the same time a social commitment to changing those sinful structures in society that deny justice, prevent peace and suppress love. In this way the doctrine of the sacrifice of the Mass can lead to the construction of a new world.

The mystery of the eucharist is also a meal. This meal is often referred to as the messianic banquet of the kingdom of God to come. In every eucharist 'by way of foretaste, we share in that heavenly liturgy which is celebrated in the holy city of Jerusalem towards which we journey as pilgrims'.[17] As a meal the elements of sharing and communing come to the fore. This sharing and communing that take place around the altar of the Lord symbolise the sharing and communing that should take place in the world around us. To share and commune with Christ our brother in the eucharist without sharing and communing with our sisters and brothers in the sanctuary of the universe would be something of a contradiction. Sacramental theology tells us that 'the sacraments effect what they signify'. The sharing and communing signified by the eucharist extends beyond the boundaries of the eucharistic community. The breaking of the bread around the altar of the Lord commits us at the same time to the breaking of earthly bread in solidarity with our sisters and brothers in the highways and byways of life. This wider sharing and communing with others, inspired and motivated by the eucharistic banquet, leads in its own way to the creation of a new world.

The mystery of the eucharist is also a memorial, not just of Calvary, but of the whole life, death and resurrection of Jesus. When we celebrate the eucharist we are responding to the command 'Do this in memory of me'. The memory of Christ which we renew in the eucharist is the memory of the living one who gave his life in love for others, a love that finds its fullest expression in his passion and death. This memorial of Christ is not simply a historical recovery of a figure from the misty past. It is a recalling of one who is already present among us in virtue of the resurrection and who is active in the community through his Spirit. The eucharist as memorial is therefore a living memorial that bodies forth and represents the dynamism of the Paschal Mystery of Christ, a dynamism that continues 'to turn the world upside down' (Acts 17:6).

The memory that we recall and that is re-presented is a memory of one who described his mission on earth in terms of:

Bringing good news to the poor,
Proclaiming release to the captives,
Recovery of sight to the blind,
Setting free those who are oppressed.

(Lk. 4:18)

The living memorial of Christ in the eucharist recalls this mission of Christ in the world which led to Cavalry and puts us in mind of our responsibilities as members of the body of Christ to continue that mission today. The eucharist as a living memorial re-activates the saving mission of Christ in the world today. The eucharist as a memorial sends out on mission those assembled in the name of Jesus, a mission that includes the liberation of humanity through social *praxis*, not as an end in itself but as a step on the way to the coming of God's Kingdom. In this sense, the eucharist as a living memorial continually puts into motion the construction of that new world for which Christ gave his life in love. Above all, the eucharist as a living memorial is also a recovery of the dangerous and disturbing memory of Jesus today. The memory of Jesus is unsettling in so far as it reminds us how God in the Christ-event put down the mighty from their thrones and exalted the lowly, filled the hungry with good things and sent the rich away empty. The memory of Jesus is the recovery of a story which is creative of a new social *praxis* directed to the poor and the needy and the outcast in the process of creating a new world.[18]

The second area mentioned by John Paul II for consideration concerns the ethical dynamism of the eucharist. It should now be clear in the light of the above remarks that bread broken without social action for justice in the world is not bread broken for a new world. The breaking of eucharistic bread demands that each participant be broken and changed in the sacrifice of the Mass so that they can go forth to build a world more in accordance with the standards of the Kingdom of God announced by Jesus. If the Christian community is to change the world, to be a leaven in society, then it must first of all be changed itself from within. That change is effected by the sacrifice of the Mass which gives rise to conversion in the life of the individual and the community, thereby enabling the community and the individual to transform the unjust structures of the world for the sake of the kingdom of God. A powerful and creative link exists between the eucharist as sacrifice, personal conversion and the Christian liberation of humanity. This means in effect that from an ethical point of view we can no longer celebrate the eucharist with eyes closed to the needs of others. The eucharist commits the individual and the Christian community to the transformation of the world. In other words, the celebration of the eucharist has both ethical presuppositions and ethical consequences. If there is no correspondence between the vision and values celebrated in the eucharist and the practical attitudes and behaviour of those participating before and after the liturgy, then a question must be raised about the sincerity and the effectiveness of that celebration of the eucharist.[19]

Furthermore, attendance at Mass is never simply an act of individual piety. It was this above all that Paul was criticising in his first letter to the Corinthians (1 Cor. 11:17–33). When we go to Mass we become part of a larger reality; we are organically incorporated into the Body of Christ. Encounter with Christ in the eucharist is never simply an encounter between me and Christ alone. It is also an encounter between the embodied Christ and the individual as a member of that particular community which is committed to continuing the mission of Christ on earth, a community committed to the creation of a better world here and now, as the matrix of the world to come.[20] This does not mean that the eucharist is now reduced to a struggle for justice or simply a sharing out of the goods of this world. Rather, the eucharist creates a community of people who together unite prayer with action, praise with justice, adoration with transformation, and contemplation with social involvement. The eucharist is that unique liturgical action which brings together into a creative but disturbing unity the vertical and horizontal dimensions of Christian mission and living. It is this unity between the celebration of the eucharist and social praxis that makes up an essential element of the ethical dynamism of the eucharist. In addition, going to Mass on Sundays is never simply the fulfilment of a personal obligation to attend Mass. Instead the celebration of the eucharist is the assumption of new responsibilities for the coming week. This is the real meaning of the Sunday obligation which must never be reduced simply to punching in forty-five minutes in the midst of many other things that have to be done at the week-end. Instead, the Sunday obligation is about the adoption and renewal of our commitment to do everything possible to change the world into a place more in accord with the Kingdom of God. These new responsibilities and obligations begin at the end of Mass when we leave to go forth, to put into practice that which we have celebrated in the Christian assembly. As such, these new responsibilities and obligations are directed to the needs of our brothers and sisters in society. They demand involvement in the work of justice, a social activity directed to the creation of a better world and the elimination of everything in society that denies the dignity of human beings.

In this regard we have something to learn from the Orthodox Church which talks about 'the liturgy after the Liturgy'. By this they mean that worship at the holy table of the Lord must flow into an act of service on the 'second altar' of freeing our needy sisters and brothers. As we have already seen, an organic unity exists, and should be seen to exist, between the eucharist and mission, between the liturgy and witness, between the Sunday assembly and the Monday world. In reality, 'the installation in history of a visible Christian fellowship which overcomes human barriers against justice, freedom and unity is a part of that liturgy after the Liturgy'.[21] There can be no doubt that the 42nd International Eucharistic Congress represented an important development, if not turning point, in the Church's understanding of the eucharist. It highlighted the indissoluble unity that exists between the breaking of eucharistic bread and the creation of a new world. It confirms the basic thesis of this final chapter — namely that there is an essential link between worship and the work of justice. In effect, action for justice is not something additional or optional or extra to the celebration of the eucharist. Rather, the work of justice is an essential and intrinsic element in every celebration of the eucharist. In view of the above arguments a strong case can be made for inserting the justice theme into the different parts of the eucharistic liturgy: the penitential rite, the homily, the prayers of the faithful, the introduction of the Lord's prayer and the final dismissal to go on mission. Equally, there is no reason why the eucharistic assembly could not from time to time become critically and creatively connected with the work of justice going on in the local community.

Lessons from Corinth for Today

By far the clearest and certainly the most significant example of the creative link that exists between the celebration of the eucharist and social praxis is given by St Paul in his first letter to the Corinthians, chapter 11. Not only does Paul argue convincingly for a new creative praxis as a result of the celebration of the eucharist but he also goes on in chapter 12 to show how this social praxis is grounded in the organic unity that exists among the many members of the one Body of Christ. The close relationship that we saw emerging in chapter four between social praxis and ontological process is exemplified by Paul in his first letter to the Corinthians. The organic unity of life challenges humanity to a liberating social praxis, and social praxis holds out the promise of determining the direction of life's social and political processes. The celebration of the eucharist calls for a new liberating praxis (chapter 11) and this liberating praxis is justified by the organic wholeness that exists among the many members that make up the Body of Christ (chapter 12).[22]

In chapter 11 of First Corinthians Paul complains about the fact that when the Christian community comes together to celebrate the eucharist there are divisions among the assembly (v. 18). For Paul, these divisions are quite incompatible with the authentic celebration of the eucharist. Indeed, he explicitly states that when such divisions exist 'it is not the Lord's supper you eat' (v. 20). As a corrective Paul reminds the Corinthians of the institution of the eucharist by Christ, placing particular emphasis on the words:

'This is my body which is for you.
Do this in remembrance of me.' (v. 24)

In the light of this teaching from Christ, Paul goes on to warn the Corinthians that

Anyone who eats and drinks without discerning the body, eats and drinks judgment upon himself. (v. 29)

Failure to discern the body can give rise to weakness, illness and even death for some (v. 30). Paul concludes this exhortation on the eucharist by recommending the Corinthians to examine their consciences when they come together to celebrate the eucharist (v. 28).

In chapter 12 Paul notes that:

> just as the body is one and has many members, and all members of the body, though many, are one, so it is with Christ. (v. 12)

For Paul, the crucial point is that the organic unity among the many members of the one Body of Christ has been established by all who 'were . . . baptised into one body . . . and were made to drink of one spirit' (v. 13). Paul unhesitatingly adopts the biological model to describe the organic unity that results from our relationship with Christ through one and the same Spirit:

> If one member suffers, all suffer together; if one member is honoured, all rejoice together. Now you are the Body of Christ and individual members of it. (vv. 26—7)

Paul's theology is so rich here that we must take a deeper look at what he is saying not only because of its importance for the question of the eucharist and social justice but also because of its affinity with one of the basic themes of this book, namely the interplay that exists between praxis and process. A number of questions need to be answered before we can appreciate the radical character of Paul's perception of the unity that exists between social praxis and ontological process as grounded in the celebration of the eucharist. What kind of meals were taking place at Corinth? What is the meaning of the expression 'discerning the body'? What is the overriding context of Paul's remarks? What are the implications of his understanding of the organic unity of the Body of Christ?

The structure of the eucharistic meal in question at Corinth seems to have been two-fold. There was an *agape* meal which seems in Corinth to have been enclosed by a blessing of the bread beforehand and the blessing of the wine afterwards. We are therefore dealing with two meals, namely the communal *agape* meal and the Lord's supper, which took place in that order. The principal problem for Paul was that some were eating the *agape* meal as if it had no relationship with the Lord's supper:

> each one goes ahead with his own meal and one is hungry and another is drunk. (v. 21)

Paul objects to this dichotomy between the two meals. The only way to correct this abuse was to remind the Corinthians of what Christ had done at the institution of the eucharist.

Paul recalls how Jesus took bread, gave thanks, broke the bread and said:

> 'This is my body,
> Do this in remembrance of me.' (v. 24)

Clearly these words of Jesus bring us to the nub of the problem at Corinth that Paul was addressing. The way we understand these words of Jesus will influence our understanding of Paul's remarks about the importance of discerning the body (v. 29).

Certainly the more traditional understanding of the words of Jesus has been to see the first *this* as referring to the bread:

> 'This (bread) is my body which is for you.'

When this is taken as the presumed interpretation then Paul's remarks about 'discerning the body' are understood to be an injunction to recognise the real presence of Christ in the eucharistic species of the blessed bread.

This particular interpretation of 1 Corinthians 11:24, 29 has been questioned in recent times for a number of reasons. In general, some see it more as 'a reading into' the text the spirit of later controversies than 'a reading out of' the text the original meaning. In particular, others point out that the Greek word used for *this* in both instances is a neuter demonstrative and therefore can hardly be taken to refer primarily to the bread which is masculine in the Greek. Further, it is noted that this neuter demonstrative (this) in Paul's writings usually refers to a larger reality when it is not specified by a neuter noun. In view of this ambiguity surrounding the first *this* we must therefore turn to the second *this*. Examination of the command 'Do this', an expression which occurs elsewhere in both the Old Testament and the New Testament, suggests that the *this* in question refers to the whole liturgical action of table fellowship rather than simply to one particular aspect of the eucharist.[23]

In the light of these observations it would seem that the import of the words of Jesus at the institution of the eucharist, quoted by Paul in his address to the Corinthians, is that

> 'your fellowship at this meal in remembrance of me is my body for you.'[24]

In other words, the emphasis appears not simply in the eucharistic species of the blessed bread but on the new body of fellowship effected by eating the eucharistic bread. It is this new corporate reality brought about by the eucharist that is the real presence of the Body of Christ. This particular social and corporate understanding of the presence of Christ in the eucharistic assembly is borne out by Paul's earlier comment to the Corinthians in chapter 10:7:

> The bread that we break, is it not a participation in the Body of Christ. Because there is one bread, we who are many are one body, for we partake of the one bread.

For Paul, therefore, it is not just the bread alone which is being called the Body of Christ but the community of people drawn and assembled together as a new reality in sharing the eucharistic species. Paul is quite insistent throughout his writings in asserting the profound, organic unity that exists in the Body of Christ between the Head and members (1 Cor. 6:4; 1 Cor. 12:13–27; Ep. 5:29–30). Any suggestion that the Body of Christ could be divided into separate parts is contrary to the spirit of Paul's theology.

In the light of these observations it becomes quite clear that Paul's remarks about 'discerning the body' do not refer primarily to recognising the real presence of Christ in the eucharistic species. Indeed the fact that the Corinthians were coming together specifically to celebrate the eucharist was in itself an indication that they already recognised the real presence of Christ in the eucharistic species. Instead Paul's plea for the Corinthians to discern the body was an injunction to recognise the full Body of Christ in the organic unity of the Head and members. Paul is concerned above all to keep together as a single organic reality the constitutive elements of the Body of Christ — namely the Head and members, the eucharistic elements and the community. To discern the whole body is to recognise the indissoluble link that pertains between the eucharistic action and the new community that is created in the performance of that action.

Paul's primary complaint therefore in his letter to the Corinthians consisted in the fact that they were dichotomising the eucharistic presence of Christ from the presence of Christ in the community. In effect the Corinthians were separating the Head and members of the one Body of Christ. This dichotomy was giving rise to the existence of a disembodied Christ, a concept completely alien to the mind-set of Paul. The Christ of Paul's theology is primarily a corporate Christ, a Christ who is organically present in and among the community of his followers. This strong sense of the organic unity of the different members of Christ is grounded in Paul's theology of baptism (Rom. 6:3ff. and Gal. 3:27–28), the unifying effect of the outpouring of the Spirit among the diverse members of the one Body of Christ (1 Cor. 12:13) and Paul's radical perception of the one-ness of all in the Body of Christ. Because the Corinthians had separated the Head from the members, Christ from the community, they could go ahead with the so-called *agape* meal without taking into account the needs of others. Once the reality of Christ becomes disembodied, the primacy and importance of social praxis is diminished within the Christian community.

The immediate background to this abuse was the presence among some in Corinth of an incipient gnosticism[25] i.e. a tendency to reduce faith in Christ to a form of esoteric saving knowledge. As a result the corporate dimension of the presence of Christ was played down. Thus, in another part of the letter to the Corinthians we find Paul complaining:

'Do you not know that your bodies are members of Christ?'   (1 Cor. 6:14)

Within Corinth some were focusing attention on the glorified, heavenly Christ to the neglect of the corporate presence of Christ on earth. Another factor, also closely connected with this gnostic orientation, was the tendency to over-spiritualise the doctrine of the in-dwelling of the Holy Spirit. This resulted in a neglect of the social dimension of Christian faith and a corresponding failure to take seriously the implications of Paul's thinking about the corporate body of Christ on earth. A dichotomy between the spiritual and the social, between the sacred and the secular, between the private and the public begins to take place which minimises the responsibility of the Christian community. A third element underlying the abuses at the celebration of the Lord's supper was the presence at Corinth of a tendency towards individualism. This tendency showed a complete insensitivity to the fact that they were all members of one another 'in Christ' and should therefore act accordingly. Thus, Paul has to remind them:

that no one should seek his own good but the good of his neighbour.   (1 Cor. 10:24)

Because of the deviations taking place — namely the gnostic tendency accompanied by a form of verticalism, spiritualism and individualism, the Corinthians could come together to celebrate the eucharist and remain oblivious of the social implications of what they were doing. In particular they could come together for the express purpose of celebrating the eucharist and yet proceed to eat and drink the *agape* meal in a manner that was divisive and neglectful of the needs of others, and in the next moment celebrate the Lord's supper as if the Christ present in the eucharist (the Head) was totally absent in the body of the faithful (the members).

What is perhaps both fascinating and disturbing is that it is these same background factors operating in Corinth that seem to characterise many of our contemporary celebrations of the eucharist. We have already seen in chapter four how individualism, spiritualism and privatisation are some of the outstanding qualities of contemporary society. It is the prevalence of these elements that lies behind the breakdown in the creative link that should exist between the celebration of the eucharist and action for social justice today in our Sunday assemblies. The problems at Corinth concerning the celebration of the eucharist are very close to the problems of the twentieth century in first world celebrations of the eucharist. They are basically problems of individualism, spiritualism and privatisation of Christian faith. To this extent we have much to learn today from a close reading of Paul's first letter to the Corinthians. In particular we have much to discover from Paul's strong theology of the organic unity that exists in the Body of Christ between the Head and members and the particular demands that this makes upon us in terms of social praxis. We too, like the Corinthians, need to discern the Body of Christ in our celebration of the eucharist. Above all, we too, like the Corinthians, must examine our social consciences when it comes to the celebration of the eucharist. 'Let a man examine himself, And so eat of the bread and drink of the cup'. (v. 28) The object of that examination of conscience must be the social implications of being a member of the Body of Christ through the eucharistic action of eating the bread and sharing the cup of eternal life.

It is quite clear that Paul is concerned in First Corinthians, chapter 11, 'with the blindness and poverty of social interaction'[26] taking place at Corinth in the context of the celebration of the eucharist. His purpose in the same chapter, verses 17ff. is 'to achieve a greater social integration'.[27] It is precisely these same issues that are in question in our contemporary celebration of the eucharist: a lack of attention to social praxis, a neglect of social justice, the need for social interaction and integration in virtue of our membership in the one Body of Christ.

This strong sense of social cohesion that exists in the Body of Christ in virtue of the eucharist is further supplemented by Paul in chapter 12 of First Corinthians. He argues that it is 'one and the same Spirit' (1 Cor. 12:11) that gives a variety of gifts to the Christian community which always works towards 'the common good' (1 Cor. 12:7). Equally all have been baptised by 'the one Spirit' into the 'one body' (1 Cor. 12:12). This radical unity 'in Christ' is compared by Paul to the organic unity that exists among the different parts that make up the human body all working together:

> As it is, there are many parts, yet one body. The eye cannot say to the hand, 'I have no need of you'. On the contrary, parts of the body which seem to be weaker are indispensable. (1 Cor. 12:21–22)

This biological image brings out the kind of unity, dependence and interdependence that should exist among the many members of the one Body of Christ; a unity, dependence and interdependence that is reminiscent of many elements of Whitehead's processive philosophy of organism. For Paul, there is a fundamental 'relational wholeness' among the many members of the one Body of Christ.[28] This 'relational wholeness' of Paul that exists in the Body of Christ resembles in many respects Whitehead's understanding of the organic unity of the whole universe: 'There is one whole, arising from the interplay of many details . . . (and) the interdependence of the one and the many.'[29] It is this 'relational wholeness' that makes serious demands in terms of social praxis on all who make up the one Body of Christ. Further, for Paul there is a radical oneness among the many different members of the Body of Christ:

> 'You are all one in Christ'
> (Gal. 3:28) since
> 'In him all things hold together'
> (Col. 1:17).

To invoke a Whiteheadian principle here one might say: 'The many become one' in Christ and 'are increased by one'.[30] This organic oneness in Christ is the foundational argument against all forms of individualism, spiritualism and privatisation in the praxis of Christian faith. The Christian, according to the Pauline scheme of things, is never alone, is never merely an individual, is never just a solitary being. Instead for Paul, the Christian in virtue of the doctrines of the Spirit, baptism and the eucharist is always a member of a wider household, is always a being-becoming-in-community, is always part of a larger reality. As John C. Haughey so aptly puts it:

> Strays become a flock. Individuals become a people. The individual stones ... become part of a living temple. 'I's' become 'we's' ... .[31]

Paul's perception of this unity in Christ as something affecting all members of the Body of Christ whether in suffering or in honour (1 Cor. 12:26) echoes very closely Whitehead's claim that local agitations have world-wide repercussions.[32] It is this radical unity, relatedness and interdependence of the whole of reality, especially the Christian community, that gives social praxis a position of primacy in the future shaping of our world today.

In conclusion to this chapter and indeed to underline the whole thrust of this book it must be pointed out that there is a close relationship between the unity of the Christian community and the unity of humanity. The Second Vatican Council taught that:

> the Church is a kind of sacrament ... of the unity of all mankind. She is also an instrument for the achievement of such . . . unity. For this reason, this Council wishes to set forth ... the encompassing mission of the Church.[33]

The Church is for the world and the eucharist nourishes the hungers of humanity. Both Church and eucharist are rooted in the vision of hope given to us by Jesus in his preaching about and praxis for the coming Kingdom of God. Action for justice that neglects the unity of the Church can hardly be termed Christian. Equally, however, a concern for the unity of the Church that turns a blind eye to the needs of the world is out of touch with the vision of Jesus. For this reason we have concluded these reflections with a strong emphasis on the sacramental, especially the sacrament of the eucharist, which mediates between the unity of the Church and unity of humanity. The sacramental life of the Church builds up the Christian community. At the same time the sacramental life of the Church has a fundamental missionary thrust to it which includes the ethical task of liberating action for justice in our world. One important way of realising this ethical task is in and through a social praxis that is sensitive to the organic-processive unity of the Church and the world. The eucharist, which is the great sacrament of unity within the Church and for the world, is an important agent of Christian liberation for the whole family of humanity. When this begins to happen then:

> . . . your sons and daughters shall prophesy,
> and young men shall see visions,
> and your old men shall dream dreams;
> Yea, and on my menservants and my
>   maidservants in those days
> I will pour out my Spirit.
>
> Acts 2:17–18.

Notes

Chapter 1
The Move to Praxis in Theology
(pp. 6—31)

1. J. Malone, 'How Effective is the Church Social Doctrine', *Origins*, 26 November 1981, 376.
2. D. Tracy, 'A Response to Fr. Metz', *Theology and Discovery: Essays in Honor of K. Rahner*, ed. W. J. Kelly (Wisconsin: Marquette University Press, 1980), 184.
3. See for example: R. McAfee Brown, *Theology in a New Key* (Philadelphia: The Westminster, 1978); A. T. Hennelly, *Theologies in Conflict: The Challenge of J. C. Segundo* (New York: Orbis Books, 1979); R. D. Johns, *Man in the World: The Theology of J. B. Metz* (Montana: Scholars Press, 1976); C. Davis, *Theology and Political Society* (Cambridge: C.U.P., 1980).
4. On the difference between political and liberation theology, see F. P. Fiorenza, 'Political and Liberation Theology: An inquiry into their Fundamental Meaning', *Liberation, Freedom and Revolution*, ed. T. E. McFadden (New York: Seabury, 1975), 3-29.
5. On the rediscovery of experience within Catholic theology see D. Lane, *The Experience of God: An Invitation to do Theology* (Dublin: Veritas Publications, 1981), ch. 1.
6. See B. Lonergan, 'The Subject', *A Second Collection*, eds. W. F. J. Ryan and B. J. Tyrell (London: Darton Longman and Todd, 1974), 69-85; K. Rahner, *Foundations of Christian Faith* (London: DLT, 1978), 26-31; J. B. Metz, *Faith in History and Society* (London: Burns and Oates, 1980), 60-70.
7. See J. B. Metz, *Faith in History and Society*, op. cit., 50-60. Other European theologians concerned with the place of *praxis* in theology would include J. Moltmann, A. Fierro, D. Soelle, and E. Schillebeeckx.
8. Ibid., 79 n.3.
9. Ibid., 157.
10. Ibid., 157-8.
11. Ibid., 65.
12. Ibid., 158-60.

13. Ibid., 161.
14. Ibid., 163.
15. This particular formulation by Metz is found in 'An Identity Crisis in Christianity?: Transcendental and Political Responses', *Theology and Discovery: Essays in Honor of K. Rahner* (Wisconsin: Marquette University Press, 1980), 170. This article is slightly expanded in Metz's book *Faith in History and Society*, op. cit., 154-68.
16. J. B. Metz, *Faith in History and Society*, op. cit., 164-5.
17. Ibid., 167 n. 15.
18. Ibid., 165.
19. Ibid., 50-1.
20. Ibid., 79 n. 5. Metz outlines more extensively the practical character of christology in *Followers of Christ* (New York: Paulist Press, 1978), ch. 2.
21. Ibid., 53. This Copernican revolution in philosophy will be examined in chapter two.
22. Ibid., 53.
23. Ibid., 54.
24. Ibid., 56-8.
25. See the constructive proposals by D. Tracy 'A Response to Fr. Metz', op. cit., 184-7; H. Lamb, *Solidarity with Victims: Towards a Theology of Social Transformation.* (New York: Crossroad, 1982) ch. 5; F. Fiorenza, 'Fundamental Theology and the Enlightenment', *The Journal of Religion*, July 1982, 289-98.
26. K. Rahner, 'Christian Humanism', *Theological Investigations*, vol. 9 (London: D.L.T., 1972), 189.
27. See L. Boff, *Jesus Christ Liberator* (New York: Orbis Books, 1978, original in Spanish in 1972); I. Sobrino, *Christology at the Crossroads* (New York: Orbis Books, 1978, original in Spanish in 1976); E. Schillebeeckx, *Christ: The Christian Experience in the Modern World* (London: S.C.M., 1977). It should be noted in fairness here that Schillebeeckx's Christology of Praxis only appeared in the same year as Metz's book *Faith in History and Society*.
28. G. Gutiérrez, *A Theology of Liberation* (New York: Orbis Books, 1973), 11. An outline of books and articles by G. Gutiérrez is available in R. McAfee Brown, *G. Gutiérrez* (Atlanta: John Knox Press, 1980), 80-4.
29. Ibid., 6-11.
30. Ibid., 11-16.
31. Available in Latin America in *Frontiers of Theology*, ed. R. Gibellini (New York: Orbis Books, 1979), 1-33.
32. 'Faith as Freedom: Solidarity with the Alienated and Confidence in the Future', *Living with Change, Experience, Faith*, ed. F. A. Eigo (Villanova: Villanova University Press, 1976), 42.
33. 'Two Theological Perspectives: Liberation Theology and Progressionist Theology', *The Emergent Gospel: Theology from the Underside of History*, ed. S. Torres and V. Fabella (New York: Orbis Books, 1978), 247.

34. 'Liberation Praxis and Christian Faith', *Frontiers of Theology*, ed. R. Gibellini, 33 n. 9.
35. Ibid., 22, 24.
36. Ibid., 23.
37. G. Gutiérrez and R. Schaul, *Liberation Theology*, ed. R. H. Stone (Atlanta: John Knox Press, 1977), 85.
38. 'Liberation Praxis and Christian Faith', op. cit., 8.
39. Ibid., 9-12. An excellent account of the theological and pastoral implications of the option for the poor, with special reference to the challenge this has for Ireland, is given by D. Carroll, 'The Option for the Poor' (*The Furrow*, November 1982), 667-79.
40. Ibid., 20, 18.
41. Ibid., 18-19.
42. Ibid., 19 and 2.
43. Ibid., 20.
44. Ibid., 23, 21.
45. 'Faith as Freedom: Solidarity with the Alienated and Confidence in the Future', op. cit., 37.
46. D. Tracy 'Introduction', *The Challenge of Liberation Theology*, eds. B. Mahan and L. D. Richesin (New York: Orbis Books, 1981), 1.
47. 'Liberation Praxis and Christian Faith', 20-21, 23; *A Theology of Liberation*, 37; 'Terrorism, Liberation, and Sexuality', *The Witness*, April 1977, 10.
48. S. Ogden, 'The Concept of a Theology of Liberation: Must a Christian Theology Today be so Conceived?' *The Challenge of Liberation Theology*, op. cit., 127-40.
49. S. Ogden, *Faith and Freedom: Toward a Theology of Liberation* (Belfast: Christian Journal Ltd., 1979).
50. S. Ogden, 'The Concept of a Theology of Liberation: Must a Christian Theology be so Conceived?' *The Challenge of Liberation Theology*, op. cit., 134, 129.
51. Ibid., 134.
52. Ibid., 131-2.
53. Ibid., 134.
54. S. Ogden, *Faith and Freedom: Toward a Theology of Liberation*, 34.
55. J. B. Metz, *Faith in History and Society*, op. cit., 212.
56. L. Boff, *Jesus Christ Liberator*, op. cit., 47.

Chapter 2
Praxis and its Philosophical Background
(pp. 32–55)

1. J. Moltmann, *The Crucified God* (New York: Harper and Row, 1974), 317.
2. H. Assman, *Theology For a Nomad Church* (New York: Orbis Books, 1976), 74. The original, and more significant title of this book was: *Teologia desde la praxis de la liberation: Ensayo*

teologico desde la America dependiente (1973).

3. The distinction between political and liberation theology is developed by F. Fiorenza in 'Political Theology and Liberation Theology', *Liberation, Revolution and Freedom*, ed. T. McFadden (New York: Seabury, 1975), 3-29.

4. D. Tracy started talking formally about 'practical theology' in contrast to other theologies in *Blessed Rage For Order* (New York: Seabury, 1975), 56 n. 1, 235 n. 101, 240-50. Tracy develops more explicitly the identity of 'practical theology' in contrast to fundamental theology and systematic theology in *The Analogical Imagination* (New York: Crossroad Publishing Company, 1981), 69-79. John A. Coleman talks about the genre of practical theology in *An American Strategic Theology* (New York: Paulist Press, 1982), 1.

5. Representatives of critical theology would include G. Baum, *Religion and Alienation* (New York: Paulist Press, 1975), ch. IX; C. Davis, *Theology and Political Society* (Cambridge: C.U.P., 1980), 24-5, 73-4.

6. B. Lonergan, 'The On-going Genesis of Methods', *Studies in Religion*, 6/4 (1977), 341, 351.

7. M. Lamb, 'The Theory-Praxis Relationship in Contemporary Christian Theologies' *C.T.S.A. Proceedings 31* (New York: Manhattan, 1976), 149-78. This article reappears, with some modifications, in Lamb's book *Solidarity With Victims* (New York: Crossroad Publishing Company, 1982), ch. 3.

8. This whole section is indebted to the magisterial work of N. Lobkowicz, *Theory and Practice: History of a Concept from Aristotle to Marx* (South Bend: University of Notre Dame Press, 1967). On the difference between *theoria, praxis* and *poiesis* see Lobkowicz 9ff.

9. N. Lobkowicz, *Theory and Practice*, op. cit., 12.

10. N. Lobkowicz, *Theory and Practice*, op. cit., 60.

11. Augustine, *City of God* (New York: Image Books, 1958), 467.

12. N. Lobkowicz, *Theory and Practice*, op. cit., 71.

13. N. Lobkowicz, *Theory and Practice*, op. cit., 73.

14. *Ordinatio*, Prologus, par. v, no. 6; ed. Vaticana I, 230.

15. R. J. Bernstein, *Praxis and Action* (Philadelphia: University of Pennsylvania Press, 1971), 7.

16. G. E. S. Anscombe, *Intention* (Oxford: Basil Blackwell, 1958), 57.

17. G. W. F. Hegel, *Reason in History* (New York: The Liberal Arts Press, 1953), 51.

18. G. W. F. Hegel, *Reason in History*, op. cit., 89.

19. R. J. Bernstein, *Praxis and Action*, op. cit., 21-2.

20. G. W. F. Hegel, *Reason in History*, op. cit., 69.

21. Ibid., 69.

22. R. J. Bernstein, *Praxis and Action*, op. cit., 35.

23. E. Simpson, 'Review Article: How Many Marxisms', *Social Theory and Practice* (Spring 1982), 116.
24. A. Gouldner, *The Two Marxisms: Contradictions and Anomalies in the Development of Theory* (New York: Seabury Press, 1980), ch. 2 at 33.
25. *Writings of the Young Marx on Philosophy and Society*, ed. L. D. Easton and K. H. Guddat (New York: Doubleday and Co., Anchor Books, 1967), 289. The expression 'political economy' in Marx means more or less what we understand by the general use of the term 'capitalism'.
26. Ibid., 414.
27. Ibid., 212.
28. Available in *Writings of the Young Marx*, 400-2.
29. This is the basic thesis of Bernstein's important study of Marx in *Praxis and Action*, 13, 76. Bernstein does not subscribe to the view that the later Marx abandoned the concept of praxis, see Bernstein 57ff.
30. On the influence of critical theory on other areas of theology see: E. Schillebeeckx, *The Understanding of Faith* (New York: Seabury Press, 1974), ch. 7; 'Critical Theories and Christian Political Commitment', *Concilium*, 84 (New York: Herder & Herder, 1974); F. Fiorenza 'Critical Social Theory and Christology' *C.T.S.A. Proceedings*, 30 (1975), 63-110.
31. A. Quinton, 'Critical Theory', *Encounter* (October 1974, London), 44.
32. See M. Jay, *The Dialectical Imagination: A History of the Frankfurt School and the Institute of Social Research, 1923-1950* (Boston: Little, Brown & Company, 1973), 51.
33. Available in H. Horkheimer, *Critical Theory* (New York: Seabury Press, 1972), 188-243.
34. Ibid., 188-9.
35. Ibid., 209-10.
36. Ibid., 233.
37. Ibid., 215.
38. H. Horkheimer, 'Zum Problem der Warheit', *Zeitschrift für Sozialforschung*, IV, 3 (1935), 345.
39. T. Adorno, *Kierkegaard: Konstruktion des Aesthetschen* (Frankfurt, 1966), 111.
40. H. Horkheimer, *Critical Theory*, 215-16, 242.
41. See T. McCarthy 'Translator's Introduction' in J. Habermas, *Legitimation Crisis* (Boston: Beacon Press, 1975), xx.
42. J. Habermas, *Theory and Practice* (Boston: Beacon Press, 1973), 254.
43. Ibid., 255.
44. J. Habermas, *Knowledge and Human Interests* (Boston: Beacon Press, 1972), vii.
45. Ibid., 303.

46. Ibid., 307.
47. Ibid., 196.
48. J. Habermas, 'A Postscript to *Knowledge and Human Interest*', *Philosophy of the Social Sciences*, 3 (1973), 176.
49. J. Habermas, *Theory and Practice*, op. cit., 8-9.
50. J. Habermas, *Knowledge and Human Interests*, op. cit., 176.
51. A more extensive account of this debate is available in D. Misgeld, 'Critical Theory and Hermeneutics: the debate between Habermas and Gadamer' in John O'Neill, ed., *On Critical Theory* (London: Heinemann, 1976).
52. J. Habermas, *Theory and Practice*, op. cit., 18.
53. J. Habermas, 'Towards a Theory of Communicative Competence', *Inquiry*, 13 (1970), 372.
54. A helpful, short account of Habermas's theory is available in T. McCarthy 'A Theory of Communicative Competence', *Philosophy of the Social Sciences*, 3 (1973), 135-56. A more elaborate commentary and detailed critique can be found in T. McCarthy's highly acclaimed book *The Critical Theory of Jürgen Habermas* (Cambridge: M.I.T. Press, 1978).
55. J. Habermas, *Theory and Practice*, op. cit., 33.
56. See R. J. Bernstein's discussion of this point in *The Restructuring of Social and Political Theory* (New York: H. B. Jovanovich, 1976), 217.
57. J. Hellesness, 'Education and the Concept of Critique', *Continuum* (Spring-Summer 1970), 40.

Chapter 3
Praxis and Contemporary Theology
(pp. 56—82)
1. R. J. Bernstein, *Praxis and Action*, op. cit., 79.
2. Ibid., 79.
3. T. McCarthy, 'Translator's Introduction', op. cit., xix.
4. K. Marx, 'Preface' in *Contribution to the Critique of Political Economy*, ed. M. Dobb (New York: International Publishers, 1970), 21.
5. J. Habermas, *Theory and Practice*, op. cit., 169.
6. A. Quinton, 'Critical Theory', *Encounter* (October 1974, London), 51.
7. M. Horkheimer in M. Horkheimer and T. Adorno, *Dialectic of Enlightenment* (New York: Herder & Herder, 1972) x. A constructive analysis of Horkheimer's exposé of this myth of 'things as they actually are' alongside Lonergan's concept of 'the Reign of Sin' can be found in W. Loewe, 'Dialectics of Sin: Lonergan's Insight and the Critical Theory of Max Horkheimer', *Anglican Theological Review*, 41/2 (1979), 224-5.
8. See N. Gottwald, *The Tribes of Yahweh. A Sociology of the Religion of Liberated Israel* (New York: Orbis Books, 1979).

9. M. Lamb, *Solidarity With Victims* (New York: Crossroad Publishing Company, 1982), 29.

10. M. Horkheimer and T. Adorno, *Dialectic of Enlightenment*, 256.

11. T. McCarthy, Translator's Introduction, op. cit., xxi.

12. Ibid., xxii.

13. J. Habermas, *Towards a Rational Society* (London: Heinemann, 1971), 112.

14. See T. Schroyer 'Marx and Habermas', *Continuum* (Spring-Summer, 1970), 54; M. Lamb, *Solidarity With Victims*, op. cit., 48.

15. L. Gilkey, *Society and the Sacred* (New York: Crossword Publishing Company, 1981), ch. 7.

16. R. J. Bernstein, *The Restructuring of Social and Political Theory*, 205-6.

17. C. Davis, *Theology and Political Society*, 95-7.

18. M. Lamb, 'The Theory-Praxis Relationship in Contemporary Christian Theologies', *C.T.S.A. Proceedings*, 31 (1976), 149-78. This article has reappeared as chapter three in Lamb's book *Solidarity With Victims* (1982). The book form of the article contains important clarifications, some of which no doubt were prompted by William Shea's article 'Seminar on Theology and Philosophy: Matthew Lamb's Five Models of Theory-Praxis and the Interpretation of John Dewey's Pragmatism', *C.T.S.A. Proceedings*, 32 (1977), 125-41, esp. 140. Here we will follow the book form of Lamb's original article.

19. Lamb's association of Lonergan with the fifth model (*Solidarity With Victims*, 103) and his suggestion that the 'work of B. Lonergan has provided ... the most decisive elaboration of the foundations of a critical praxis correlation for the doing of theology', *C.T.S.A. Proceedings*, 31 (1976), 173, is open to further discussion. To be sure Lonergan does constructively emphasise the importance of the praxis of authentic self-transcendence and its accompanying experience of personal conversion. But does Lonergan — for example in his article on 'Theology and Praxis' in *C.T.S.A. Proceedings*, 1977 or indeed in *Method in Theology* — adequately stress the importance of social, political and transformative praxis? Would Lonergan's method grant the need to reformulate doctrine on the basis of faith-inspired social and political praxis? Does Lonergan's understanding of doctrine demand social praxis? In brief, does Lonergan explicitly affirm the primacy of transformative praxis as this is understood by liberation theologians such as Gustavo Gutiérrez? Obviously, a full discussion of these questions cannot be undertaken here. A useful starting point for such a discussion might be the distinction that D. Tracy makes between the classical (Aristotelian) understanding of praxis and the Hegelian-Marxist understanding of praxis. Tracy situates Lonergan, correctly we believe, in the former category. See D. Tracy, *The Analogical Imagination*, op. cit., 69-79.

Within such a discussion reference could also be made to: (a) the important responses by M. Lamb and E. Braxton to Lonergan's article in the *C.T.S.A. Proceeding*, 32 (1977), 17-21, 22-27; (b) some aspects of C. Davis, 'Lonergan's Appropriation of the Concept of Praxis', *New Blackfriars* (1981), 114-26.

20. N. Lobkowicz, *Theory and Practice*, op. cit., 340.
21. G.E.M. Anscombe, *Intention* (Oxford: B. Blackwell, 1958), 57.
22. P. Berger and T. Luckmann, *The Social Construction of Reality* (New York: Anchor Books, 1967), 9.
23. M. Novak, *The Spirit of Democratic Capitalism* (New York: Simon and Schuster, 1982), 343-4.
24. J. B. Metz, *Faith in History and Society* (London: Burns and Oates, 1980), 121-2.
25. E. Schillebeeckx, 'Critical Theories and Christian Political Commitment', *Concilium*, 84 (New York: Herder and Herder, 1974), 50.
26. J. B. Metz, *Faith in History and Society*, 128.
27. Ibid., 129-30.
28. W. Lowe, 'Psychoanalysis and Humanism: The Permutations of Method', *C.T.S.A. Proceedings*, 34 (1979), 115.
29. T. Adorno, *Minima Moralia: Reflections on a Damaged Life* (London: New Left Books, 1974), 247.

Chapter 4
Social Analysis and Process Thought serving Praxis
(pp. 83–109)

1. Pope Paul VI, *Octogesima Adveniens*, a. 4
2. D. von Allmen, 'The Kingdom of God and Human Struggles', *Your Kingdom Come* (Geneva: W.C.C., 1980), 122.
3. J. V. Taylor, 'The Church Witnesses to the Kingdom', *Your Kingdom Come*, op. cit.
4. Quotation taken from *The Irish Times*, 27 November 1982, 18.
5. L. Gilkey, 'Can Art Fill the Vacuum?', *Criterion*, Autumn 1981, 8.
6. H. Marcuse, *An Essay on Liberation* (Middlesex: Penguin Books, 1969), 21-2.
7. A. N. Whitehead, *Process and Reality*, corrected edition (New York: The Free Press, 1978), 4 and 167 respectively.
8. Ibid., 3.
9. A. N. Whitehead, *Modes of Thought* (New York: The Free Press, 1968), 60.
10. J. Cobb, *God and the World* (Philadelphia: The Westminster Press, 1969), 70.
11. A. N. Whitehead, *Process and Reality*, op. cit., 88.
12. A. N. Whitehead, *Science and the Modern World* (New York: The Free Press, 1967), 152.
13. The principal works of F. Capra are *The Tao of Physics* (Suffolk: Fontana, 1976) and *The Turning Point* (New York: Simon and

Schuster, 1982).

14. See F. Capra, *The Tao of Physics*, op. cit., 202; *The Turning Point*, op. cit., 87.

15. See Penelope Washbourn's helpful article 'The Dynamics of Female Experience' in *Feminism and Process Thought*, ed. S. G. Davaney (New York: The Edwin Mellen Press, 1981), 83-105, esp. 93.

16. Ibid., 94, 93.

17. In affirming the androgynous approach to human identity care must be taken to avoid simply repeating or perpetuating the traditional understanding of androgyny as put forward by men. By and large the traditional understanding of androgyny does not take the feminine qualities seriously. See V. C. Saiving, 'Androgynous Life', *Feminism and Process Thought*, op. cit., 11-31.

18. Without this movement towards a higher synthesis there is a real danger that the androgynous ideal may simply continue to reinforce the status quo without any liberation for either women or men. See V. C. Saiving, art. cit., 16.

19. C. Birch and J. Cobb, *The Liberation of Life* (London: C.U.P., 1981), 80.

20. Ibid., 83.

21. F. Capra, *The Turning Point*, op. cit., 279.

22. C. Birch and J. B. Cobb, *The Liberation of Life*, 88, 95, 105.

23. For example, the theologian would want to distance himself at least from the apparent absence in process thought of an eschatological perspective on life, the seeming neglect by process thinkers of the dialectical and analogical character of all religious discourse, and the ambiguity surrounding 'God and Creativity' in parts of Whitehead's writings.

24. Although A. N. Whitehead receives only scant attention (one reference) in Capra's most recent work (*The Turning Point*) there is quite a remarkable sympathy between Whitehead's philosophy of organism and Capra's general systems view of life. The close relation that exists between process thought and feminism was the subject of an important symposium held in Harvard in 1978 and now available in published form as S. G. Davaney, ed., *Feminism and Process Thought*. The role that process philosopgy can play in developing an ecological perception of all of human existence is developed at length by John C. Cobb in various places, especially by C. Birch and J. Cobb, *The Liberation of Life*.

25. A. N. Whitehead, *Science and the Modern World*, op. cit., 109.

26. Ibid., 111.

27. A. N. Whitehead, *Modes of Thought* (New York: The Free Press, 1968), 138.

28. A. N. Whitehead, *Science and the Modern World*, op. cit., 156, 58.

29. A. N. Whitehead, *Process and Reality*, op. cit., 6.

30. A. N. Whitehead, *Science and the Modern World*, op. cit., 91.

31. E. Kraus, *The Metaphysics of Experience: A Companion To*

Whitehead's Process and Reality (New York: Fordham University Press, 1979), 13.

32. A. N. Whitehead, *Science and the Modern World*, op. cit., 195-6.
33. Ibid., 51ff., 91, 156.
34. Ibid., 51ff.
35. A. N. Whitehead, *Adventures of Ideas* (New York: The Free Press, 1967), 133.
36. A. N. Whitehead, *Process and Reality*, op. cit., 6.
37. A. N. Whitehead, *Adventures of Ideas*, op. cit., 28; *Science and the Modern World*, op. cit., 76ff.
38. A. N. Whitehead, *Adventures of Ideas*, op. cit., 31.
39. A. N. Whitehead, *Process and Reality*, op. cit., 290.
40. Ibid., 7.
41. Ibid., 21.
42. On the primacy of *praxis* within the preaching of Jesus on the Kingdom of God and for some allusions to the presence of what we today would call a process view of God implicit in this preaching see D. A. Lane, 'Jesus and the Kingdom of God', *The Living Light*, (Summer 1982), 103-4.
43. A. N. Whitehead, *Adventures of Ideas*, op. cit., 33-4.
44. Ibid., 63.
45. A. N. Whitehead, *Process and Reality*, op. cit., 23.

Chapter 5
The Church and Christ in Social Praxis
(pp. 110—140)
1. *Gaudium et Spes* (hereafter referred to as *G.S.*) a.4
2. The figure in 1978 was 780 million. cf. The World Bank, M. McNamara *Report on World Development*, 1978. A conservative estimate five years later could add another 20 million.
3. *North-South: A Programme For Survival*, Report of the W. Brandt Commission (London: Pan Books, 1980).
4. *Redemptor Hominis* (hereafter referred to as *R.H.*) a.16.
5. Quotation taken from J. L. Segundo, *Evolution and Guilt* (New York: Orbis Books, 1974), 124.
6. *G.S.*, a.1, 4, 45.
7. Ibid., a.1.
8. Ibid., a.43.
9. Ibid., a.55.
10. Ibid., a.72.
11. Ibid., a.85.
12. Ibid., a.73.
13. *Apostolicam actuositatem*, a.5.
14. *Populorum Progressio*, a.5.
15. Ibid., a.32.
16. Ibid., a.80.
17. Ibid., a.5.

18. *Medellín Conclusions*, a.1, 7
19. Ibid., a.10, 2.
20. *Octogesima Adveniens*, (hereafter referred to as *O.A.*), a.48, 51.
21. Ibid., a.42.
22. Ibid., a.48.
23. *Justice in the World* (hereafter referred to as *J.W.*), Introduction.
24. Ibid., ch. 2.
25. Pope Paul VI, 'Opening Address to 1974 Synod' *Catholic Mind* (March, 1975), 6.
26. *Catholic Mind* (March 1975), 50-1.
27. Ibid., 55.
28. *Evangelii Nuntiandi*, a.30, 31, 35, 38.
29. Paul VI in *Documentation Catholique*, 74, (1977), 307.
30, Y. Congar, *Un Peuple Messianique* (Paris: Les éditions du Cerf, 1975), 179.
31. The story is told how Mgr Pavan, at a meeting of the Commission on Justice and Peace in 1967, commenting on the continuity of papal encyclicals, especially *Populorum Progressio*, remarked 'Nothing has changed; one has simply moved from theory to practice, that is to say one no longer deduces from abstract principles; one observes reality in which one has discovered certain evangelical capacities . . .'. M-D. Chenu commenting on this story observes, 'Nothing has changed, but everything has changed', in *La 'doctrine sociale' de l'Église Comme idéologie* (Paris: Les éditions du cerf, 1979), 80.
32. This point has been argued most persuasively by Francis S. Fiorenza in 'The Church's Religious Identity and Its Social and Political Mission', *Theological Studies* (June 1982), 197-225.
33. A review of Puebla may be found in: 'The Message of Puebla in Latin America', *Pro Mundi Vita Bulletin*, October 1979; *Puebla and Beyond*, ed. J. Eagleson and P. Scharper (New York: Orbis Books) 1979.
34. I. Sobrino, 'The Significance of Puebla for the Catholic Church in Latin America', *Puebla and Beyond*, op. cit., 291.
35. 'Opening Address at the Puebla Conference' available in *Puebla and Beyond*, op. cit., 57-71 at 57.
36. Ibid., 1, 3.
37. Ibid., 1, 2-5; These concern the messiahship, divinity of Jesus and the portrayal of Jesus as a political activist.
38. Ibid., 1, 6.
39. Ibid., III, 2.
40. Ibid., III, 4.
41. Available in *Puebla and Beyond*, op. cit., 123-285.
42. Helpful commentaries on Puebla may be found in *Puebla and Beyond*; A. Vonder Perre, 'La Conference de Puebla', *Révue theologigue de Louvain*, 2, 1979.

43. General Audience, 21 February. See *The Pope Teaches* (London: C.T.S. Jan.-Feb. 1979), 73.
44. *The Pope Teaches*, op. cit., (July 1980), 196.
45. Available in *The Pope Teaches: The Pope in Central America*, 1983/4 (London: C.T.S., 1983), 62.
46. See the following helpful commentaries: J. Kavanagh, *On Human Work* (Dublin: Praedicanda Publications, 1983); G. Baum, *The Priority of Labor: A Commentary on Laborem Exercens* (New York: Paulist Press, 1982); D. Dorr, 'The New Social Enycyclical', *The Furrow* (November, 1981).
47. J. D. Crossan, *In Parable: The Challenge of the Historical Jesus*, (New York: Harper & Row, 1973), 35ff.
48. *G.S.*, a.39.
49. Ibid., a.38.
50. Ibid., a.39.
51. D. P. Gray, *Jesus: The Way to Freedom* (Minnesota: St Mary's Press, 1979), 12.
52. See P. Henriot, 'Social sin and Conversion: A Theology of the Church's social involvement', *Chicago Studies*, XI (1972), 3-18.
53. *G.S.*, a.25; *Medellín Conclusions*, 2, 16; 2, 1; *J.W.*, Introduction and Part III; Canadian Catholic Bishops, 'Sharing National Income', *Catholic Mind* (Oct. 1972), 59; Irish Catholic Bishops, *The Work of Justice* (Dublin: Veritas Publications, 1977), a.114, 116-18.
54. The warning against inflating the social mission of the Church is constructively made by Langdon Gilkey in *Reaping the Whirlwind: A Christian Interpretation of History* (New York: Seabury Press, 1978), 236, 236 n.126.
55. V. Cosmao develops extensively this theme in *Changer le monde: Une Tache pour l'Église*, (Paris: Les éditions du cerf, 1979).
56. *The Pope Speaks*, op. cit., (July 1980), 202.
57. The phrase is taken from J. B. Metz, 'For a Renewed Church before a New Council: A Concept in Four Theses' in D. Tracy, (ed.), *Toward Vatican III*, (New York: Seabury Press, 1978), 143ff.
58. A. N. Whitehead, *Adventures of Ideas* (New York: The Free Press, 1967, (paperback edition), 274.
59. *The Tablet* (20 Oct. 1979), 1031.
60. General Audience, 21 February 1979. See *The Pope Speaks*, op. cit., (Jan.—Feb. 1979), 74.
61. A helpful and fuller discussion of this question may be found in J. Roach, 'The Need for Public Dialogue on Religion and Politics', *Origins* (3 December 1981), 390-3 and E. McDonagh, *The Demands of Simple Justice* (Dublin: Gill and Macmillan, 1980), 29-39.
62. U.S. Bishops 'The Challenge of Peace: God's Promise and Our Response', *Origins* (19 May 1983), 13.
63. The religious dimension of politics is well described by Langdon

Gilkkey, in *Reaping the Whirlwind*, op. cit., 56: 'The deepest question of ordinary political experience has . . . a religious dimension . . . because on the one hand . . . it points to the religious fear of fate and to the religious promise of a universal destiny, to a sovereignty that can conquer fate and to the hope for an authentic history. On the other hand, it is religious because it apprehends a "fall", a warping of what is natural and normal in time — and so a need for redemption.'

64. F. S. Fiorenza, 'The Church's Religious Identity and its Social and Political Mission', *Theological Studies* (June 1982), 219.
65. See D. Tracy, *The Analogical Imagination*, op. cit., ch. 1.
66. *G.S.*, a.69.
67. Ibid., a.77.
68. *J.W.*, ch. 2.
69. *O.A.*, a.37.
70. Ibid.

Chapter 6
The Eucharist and the Praxis of Social Justice
(pp. 141–169)

1. J. Gelineau, 'Celebrating the Paschal Liberation' *Concilium* (February 1974), 107. George Higgins, the well-known American Church expert on labour issues, tells the story: 'Shortly after World War II an extremely well-informed German priest told me, on what I am prepared to accept as reliable evidence, that the Nazis, far from being worried about the pre-war growth of the liturgical movement in Germany, secretly encouraged it. According to my informant, they felt that an intense preoccupation with the liturgy would serve to distract the attention of Catholics and make them less inclined to engage in political action. Whether this report is accurate or not, the record will show, I think, that some of the most actively engaged in the liturgical movement not only in Germany but in other countries as well, did make the mistake of ignoring political and social problems or, even of at least passively favouring political programs which they should have actively opposed,' in 'The Mass and Political Order', *Proceedings of the Liturgical Conference*, Worcester, Mass., August 1955, 130-1.
2. See J. Moltmann, 'The Feast of Freedom', *The Open Church: Invitation to a Messianic Life-Style* (London: S.C.M., 1978), 64-81 at 66-72.
3. X. Léon-Dufour, 'Faites céla en memoire de moi', *Etudes* (June 1981), 840.
4. S. M. Schneiders, 'The Foot-Washing (Jn. 13/1-20): An Experiment in Hermeneutics', *Catholic Biblical Quarterly* (January 1981), 81.
5. John Chrysostom, Homily 50, Mt. Ev., 3-4, in *Patrologia Graeca*, 58, 508ff.

6. See ch. 5, section on 'Teaching of the Church since Vatican II'.
7. 'Doctrinal Agreement on the Eucharist', available in *Modern Eucharistic Agreement* (London: S.P.C.K., 1973), 61.
8. 'Pastoral Agreement', *Modern Eucharistic Agrement*, op. cit., 66.
9. John Paul II, *The Holy Eucharist* (Vatican: Polyglot Press, 1980).
10. The official proceedings of the 42nd International Eucharistic Congress are now available in *Eucharistie: Vers un monde nouveau* (Paris: Éditions du Centurion, 1981). A selection of addresses and homilies has been edited by Seán Swayne and published as *Eucharist For a New World* (Carlow: Irish Institute of Pastoral Liturgy, 1981).
11. A preparatory theological document on this theme was made available in advance of the Congress, entitled *Jesus Christ, pain rompu pour un monde nouveau*, (Éditions du Centurion, 1980).
12. *L'Osservatore Romano*, English edition (26 February 1979), 6.
13. Ibid., 10.
14. Ibid.
15. Ibid.
16. *Gaudium et Spes*, a.39.
17. *Sacro Sanctum Concilium*, a.8.
18. This particular theme is developed at greater length by J. B. Metz, *Faith in History and Society*, ch. 11.
19. G. Wainwright, *Doxology: A Systematic Theology* (London: Epworth Press, 1980), 399.
20. *Gaudium et Spes*, a.38.
21. I. Bria, 'The liturgy after the Liturgy', *Martyria/Mission: The Witness of the Orthodox Churches Today*, ed. I. Bria (Geneva: W.C.C. 1980), 70.
22. A most helpful theological commentary on First Corinthians, chapters eleven and twelve is given by John C. Haughey in 'Euchar-ist at Corinth: You are the Christ', *Above Every Name: The Lordship of Christ and Social Systems*, ed. T. E. Clarke (New York: Paulist Press, 1980), 107-33.
23. See W. F. Orr and James A. Walther, *1 Corinthians: A New Translation*, The Anchor Bible (New York: Doubleday, 1976), 271-3; J. C. Haughey, 'Eucharist at Corinth: You are the Chirst', *Above Every Name*, op. cit., 119-20.
24. J. C. Haughey, 'Eucharist at Corinth: You are the Christ', *Above Every Name*, op. cit., 119.
25. H. Conzelmann, *A Commentary on the First Epistle to the Corinthians* (Philadelphia: Fortress Press, 1975), 15.
26. J. C. Haughey, 'Eucharist at Corinth: You are the Christ', *Above Every Name*, op. cit., 117.
27. G. Theissen, 'Social Integration and Sacramental Activity: An Analysis of 1 Cor. 11: 17-34' in G. Theissen, *The Social Setting of Pauline Christianity* (Philadelphia: Fortress Press, 1982), 167.
28. J. C. Haughey, 'Eucharist at Corinth: You are the Christ', *Above*

Every Name, op. cit., 122. It should be noted that Paul is by no means alone in emphasising the organic, inclusive and relational character of Christianity. The same kind of organic vision is found in the Gospel of John who talks about the mutual indwelling of God the Father in Christ and of Christ (and the Spirit) in his followers (Jn. 14), and then goes on to employ the image of the unity of the vine and the branches to get across this strong sense of organic belongingness (Jn. 15).

29. A. N. Whitehead, *Modes of Thought*, op. cit., 60. In *Science and Modern World* Whitehead points out how his philosophy of organism 'involves the entire abandonment of the notion of simple location. In a certain sense, everything is everywhere at all times, for every location involves an aspect of itself in every other location', 91. Above all, for Whitehead 'Actuality is through and through togetherness . . .'.

30. A. N. Whitehead, *Process and Reality*, op. cit., 21, 145.

31. J. C. Haughey, 'Eucharist at Corinth: You are the Christ', *Above Every Name*, op. cit., 122.

32. A. N. Whitehead, *Modes of Thought*, op. cit., 138.

33. *Lumen Gentium*, a.1.

Select Bibliography from 1980

Ambler, R., and Haslam, D. (eds.), *Agenda for Prophets*, London: Bowerdean Press, 1980.

Baum, G., *Catholics and Canadian Socialism: Political Thoughts in the Thirties and Forties*, New York: Paulist Press, 1980.

Berwick, P., and Burns, M., *Conference on Poverty: Papers of the Kilkenny Conference 6th–8th November*, Dublin: The Council for Social Welfare, 1982.

Birch, C., and Cobb, J. B., *The Liberation of Life: From Cell to Community*, Cambridge: C.U.P., 1981/New York: C.U.P., 1981.

Bonino, J. M., *Towards a Christian Political Ethics*, London: S.C.M. Press, 1983/Philadelphia: Fortress Press, 1983.

Brown, D., *To Set at Liberty: Christian Faith and Human Freedom*, New York: Orbis Books, 1981.

Capra, F., *The Turning Point: Science, Society and the Rising Culture*, New York: Simon and Schuster, 1982.

Church of England, *The Church and the Bomb: Nuclear Weapons and Christian Conscience*, London: Hodder & Stoughton, 1982.

Clarke, T. E., *Above Every Name: The Lordship of Christ and Social Systems*, New York: Paulist Press, 1980.

Cobb, J. B., *Process Theology as Political Theology*, Manchester: Manchester U.P., 1982/Philadelphia: Westminster Press, 1982.

Cobb, J. B., and Schroeder, W. W., (eds.), *Process Philosophy and Social Thought*, Chicago: Center for Scientific Study of Religion, 1981.

Coleman, J., *An American Strategic Theology*, New York: Paulist Press, 1982.

Curran, C. E., *American Catholic Social Ethics: Twentieth Century Approaches*, Indiana: University of Notre Dame Press, 1982.

Davaney, S. G. (ed.), *Feminism and Process Thought*, New York: Edwin Mellen Press, 1981.

Davis, C., *Theology and Political Society*, Cambridge: C.U.P., 1980/New York: C.U.P., 1980.

Dorr, D., *Option for the Poor: A Hundred Years of Vatican Social Teaching*, Dublin: Gill and Macmillan, 1983/New York: Orbis Books, 1983.

German Bishops, *Out of Justice, Peace*, Joint Pastoral Letter of West

186 *Foundations for a Social Theology*

German Bishops, 1983, Dublin: Irish Messenger Publications, 1983.

Gilkey, L., *Society and the Sacred: Towards a Theology of Culture in Decline*, New York: Crossroad, 1981.

Gill, R., *Prophecy and Praxis: The Social Function of the Churches*, London: M. Morgan & Scott, 1981.

Gutiérrez, G., *The Power of the Poor in History*, London: S.C.M., 1983/New York: Orbis Books, 1983.

Irish Bishops, *The Storm that Threatens*, Dublin: Catholic Press and Information Office, 1983.

Lamb, M., *Solidarity with Victims: Towards a Theology of Social Transformation*, New York: Crossroad, 1982.

Lash, N., *A Matter of Hope: A Theologian's Reflections on the Thoughts of Karl Marx*, London: Darton Longman & Todd, 1981/Indiana: University of Notre Dame Press, 1981.

McAffee Brown, R., *Making Peace in the Global Village*, Philadelphia: Westminster Press, 1981.

McDonagh, E., *The Making of Disciples: Tasks of Moral Theology*, Dublin: Gill and Macmillan, 1982/New York: Michael Glazier, 1982.

McGovern, A.F., *Marxism: An American Christian Perspective*, New York: Orbis Books, 1981.

Mackey, J. P., *The Christian Experience of God as Trinity*, London: S.C.M., 1983.

Mahon, B., and Richesin, L. D., (eds.), *The Challenge of Liberation Theology*, New York: Orbis Books, 1981.

Meeks, W.A., *The First Urban Christians: The Social World of the Apostle Paul*, Yale: Y.U.P., 1983.

Metz, J. B., *Faith in History and Society: Towards a Practical Fundamental Theology*, London: Burns and Oates, 1980/New York: Crossroad, 1979.

Metz, J. B., *The Emergent Church: The Future of Christianity in a Postbourgois World*, London: S.C.M., 1981/New York: Crossroad, 1981.

Ogden, S., *The Point of Christology*, New York: Harper & Row, 1982.

Pixley, G. V., *God's Kingdom: A Guide for Biblical Study*, London: S.C.M., 1981/New York: Orbis Books, 1981.

Radford Ruether, Rosemary, *Sexism and God-talk: Towards a Feminist Theology*, London: S.C.M., 1983/Boston: Beacon, 1983.

Rottenberg, I.C., *The Promise and the Presence: Towards a Theology of the Kingdom of God*, Michigan: W. B. Eerdams, 1980.

Schüssler Fiorenza, Elizabeth, *In Memory of Her: a Feminist Theological Reconstruction of Christian Origins*, London: S.C.M. 1983/New York: Crossroad, 1983.

Searle, M., *Liturgy and Social Justice*, Minnesota: Liturgical Press, 1980.

Senior, D., and Stuhlmuellr, C., *Biblical Foundations for Mission*, London: S.C.M., 1983/New York: Orbis Books, 1983.

Shinn, R. L., (ed.), *Faith and Science in an Unjust World: Report of* the *W.C.C. Conference on Faith, Science and the Future*, Geneva: W.C.C., 1980.

Tracy, D., *The Analogical Imagination: Christian Theology and the Culture of Pluralism*, London: S.C.M., 1982/New York: Crossroad, 1981.

U.S. Bishops, *The Challenge of Peace: God's Promise and Our Response* in *Origins*, 19 May 1983, London: CTS/SPCK, 1983.

W.C.C. Report on Mission and Evangelism, *Your Kingdom Come: Mission Perspective*, Geneva: W.C.C., 1980.

Index